DEC 2007

MARTHA RILEY COMMUNITY
LIBRARY   ARK

W9-CQZ-832

VEGETABLES
BY 40 GREAT FRENCH CHEFS

VEGETABLES

NDSAY AND PATRICK MIKANOWSKI   JOËL THIÉBAULT • PHOTOGRAPHY GRANT SYMON

BY 40 GREAT FRENCH CHEFS

CONTENTS

the chefs

INTRODUCTION

A book about how vegetables should be grown, cooked, and eaten with passion

A few truck farms are still left in the Île-de-France, the region around Paris, but why choose Joël's? What's so special about this guy? What makes his vegetables so different? Can a book about a man who grows vegetables in the heartland of France be interesting enough to satisfy the curiosity of readers who live in distant lands under different skies?

This is an attempt to provide answers to all those questions. The truck farmer or market gardener of the Île-de-France who runs a booth at the local farmers' market has become something of a rarity.

What is becoming even rarer is someone who grows the vegetables that he sells. When you hold down two jobs at once, daily life, which is complex and stressful enough at the best of times, becomes even tougher. In his job, there is always backbreaking work to be done. The earth has to be worked by hand, which means lots of bending; the crates are heavy and have to be hauled from field to market.

Joël Thiébault is a truck farmer and vegetable aficionado, so it is perfectly logical that the recipes for the thirty-six vegetables that constitute the second part of this book have been created by equally enthusiastic cooks

Joël's ability to "wear two hats" is one that is deeply admired by the many people who shop at his market stand every week and who have been his loyal customers for many years. They know that the changing seasons and vagaries of the weather in this part of France leave their mark on the produce available on the grower's market table. The produce can be summarized generally as consisting of root vegetables in winter and leafy vegetables in summer.

Growers and customers live under the same skies, experiencing the same weather at the same time of year. So when shoppers complain of slightly blemished leaves, a legacy of the previous week's rain, he or she is told, "Remember, it rained quite heavily six days ago," and the customers will think back to the showers that darkened the city streets and forced them to open an umbrella. Despite the weather and peer pressure, there has been no spraying with chemicals to prevent damage; however, that has done nothing to spoil the flavor. And after all, as long as a whole army of slugs and snails has not invaded the territory, it's not so terrible if a few of the leaves are a little ragged.

Traceability—the word is on everyone's lips, but it's hard to practice due to the convolutions of globalized production. Yet it's being practiced right here by the shoppers at the local farmers' market, and they are scarcely conscious of doing it, like the poet who doesn't know it.

Does traceability mean sharing the same weather as the man who sells you your vegetables?

No, but it sure is a big help. It may not be enough, for the pleasure of eating good food and providing oneself with an iron constitution, to strictly check how your vegetables are grown, transported, and sold. You need to talk to the grower himself and learn something about his environment. That will give you an extra source of information.

What a pleasure it is to discover that behind the trestle tables stands someone who will not only give you a wealth of information about the way his vegetables have been grown, but also advise you about the best way to prepare, cook, and use them, as well as how to store them in a way that keeps them as fresh as possible. After all, you don't have time to shop for food every day. Joël can teach you a whole way of eating if you'll take the time to stop and listen, even if this means waiting in line. So be patient, and take time to look over the produce carefully before asking questions.

This book is a tribute to all the small farmers who till the soil every day and in all weather, but it's also a useful guide for enthusiastic kitchen gardeners. For those who will never get the chance to visit with Joël at the market booth, it will also provide a taste of his hard work.

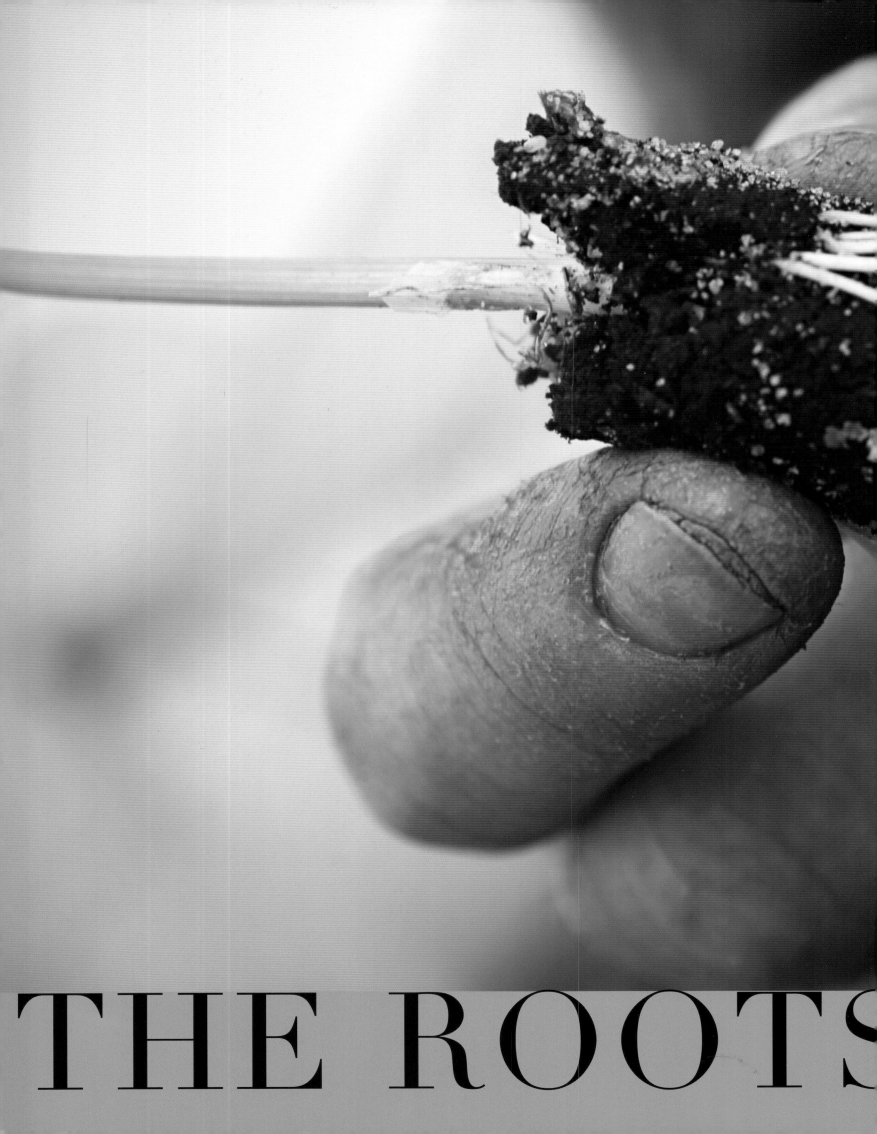

THE ROOTS

OF PASSION

Plate from the catalog of Vilmorin-Andrieux & Co. (c. 1876).

Tying spring turnips into bunches.

A bunch of Milan spring turnips.

Creating a portrait of Joël Thiébault, **one of France's most gifted vegetable growers, means describing the many aspects of his work, and explaining the history of his family and the place they occupy in the story of vegetable-growing in the Île-de-France; it also involves explaining the past and present of this traditional occupation. On the land he owns beside the Seine, west of Paris, Joël grows varieties of vegetables and herbs, some of whose shapes and flavors date from far back in time, though they have traveled a long way from their origins.**

Roger Thiébault, Joël's father (1929–1994), returning home after plowing.

In one year, Joël may grow more than 1,600 varieties of herbs and vegetables

Joël has been a grower for nearly twenty-five years. Why did he become a truck farmer, a market gardener? Was it just because he enjoyed it? Was he crazy about vegetables? Yes, no doubt, but would that have been enough to make him work in the mud and the icy cold of a frosty winter's day? Because that's what he has to do when he's lifting turnips or picking cabbages and leeks. And in high summer, who wants to spend time walking up and down along the polytunnels, in which tender shoots are cultivated to protect them from the extremes of cold and moisture? The enormous lengths of semi-transparent polyethylene are laid over hoops that can be as high as 10 feet at the apex. Inside the tunnel, the air is stifling and humid, soon becoming unbearable if the weather is even mildly sunny.

There is no other way to grow semi-tropical crops such as tomatoes and eggplant, whose fragile, brilliantly colored fruits have to be picked at first light—this means at dawn in

the summer, so around 6:00 A.M. But the quality of these vegetables will send shoppers at that day's market into transports of delight. That's because Joël not only grows his vegetables, he sells them as well. He could have been content with leading a country life, tending a kitchen garden in a sheltered backwater, and leaving the sale of his vegetables to a distribution circuit run by people he would never meet who would sell his produce in bulk.

But that's not how it is, because Joël loves to sells his vegetables in the street markets of Paris, where there is a unique, relaxed atmosphere of simplicity and good manners that is so characteristic of the way he welcomes his customers. He takes immense pleasure in giving them advice, explaining the lore and legend of the vegetables on his cart, many of which are unusual forms of old favorites. For instance, how about a bright golden beet, a striped red-and-green tomato, or dark red carrots? These would be greeted elsewhere with a grimace, so deeply is food conservatism ingrained in us. But here, there is little hesitation; doubts are quickly brushed aside by Joël's enthusiasm. His praises are sung by the chefs of the starred restaurants who seek out his produce, thus dispelling the last shred of prejudice.

Joël pursues his occupation from a position of encyclopedic knowledge. He is passionate about cultivated edible plants, he knows their horticultural requirements and their history. He has an insatiable curiosity and cannot resist cultivating a new species or reintroducing an ancient cultivar or variety. To do this, he needs to find out as much as he can about it, acquiring information from other growers, collecting names and, when the crop has been harvested for the first time, getting friends who are chefs and cooks to try it out and pronounce their verdict.

Know-how and skills are also required for managing a truck farm that employs around ten people and for running two market booths four times a week. Socializing and doing the accounts also take time, so he may find himself working until the wee hours. The evenings are spent on administration. Faxes must be sent and emails arrive in droves and must be answered; the restaurant chefs are ending their shifts and are eager to place their orders for the following day.

Joël thus perpetuates the tradition of the generations of growers who have toiled on the outskirts of Paris to supply the citizens of what was once one of the largest cities in the world

The fields of grain, the kitchen gardens, the orchards, and the herds of sheep and cattle supplied the markets of the French capital, and had to do so on a daily basis, until the advent of modern methods of transportation, especially the railroad, in the nineteenth century. Parisians have always had a reputation for being discerning gourmets. Those who buy their vegetables from Joël are upholding the tradition. From celebrity chefs running five-star restaurants, and hard-working bistro cooks laboring nightly over hot stoves, to the most discerning gourmets, Parisians make the weekly journey from the Left Bank to the Right, or drive long distances around the ring road, the Boulevard Péripherique, in search of Joël Thiébault's produce. They know that they will always find what they are looking for at Joël's. Joël is surrounded by a faithful team of cousins—and cousins of cousins—from Portugal, an extended family who give him constant support. He is the scion of a long line of truck farmers who have farmed at Carrières-sur-Seine since the Middle Ages. If he considers his work to be a matter of honor and sharing, as befits a true aristocrat, it is because his genealogical tree is that of a prince of the kitchen garden. Joël Thiébault has always considered it important to carry on the family tradition, always trying to improve. His day begins early and seems almost endless, as proven by the freshness and variety of his produce. •••

The young shoots of the Morgane bean.

Joël, how do you fertilize your soil?

"Even though it's hard to generalize when it comes to nutritional requirement, NPK report 3/2/6 reveals a little of the way in which I grow my produce. Nitrogen-rich fertilizer might make my vegetables into 'racehorses,' too highly strung to resist the changeable weather, and phosphates are little needed because our truck-farm soils are rich in them and vegetables only use them at the start of their growth. I feed them potassium, or rather potassium oxide in the form of potassium sulfate, because sulfur is vital for vegetables. This balance has given us plants that are better equipped to resist fungal diseases, insect pests, and even early frosts in the fall. Greater ground cover in the winter enables us to fix the remains of the fertilizers and prevent run-off of the chemicals that pollute the water table."

A bouquet of spring chive flowers.

What's the point of all that effort? Why take so much trouble, and do research to achieve quality just for the pleasures of the table ?

Not only does Joël love his job, he also loves food! He is the first to notice when his turnips have turned pink or golden, he revels in the sweetness of his garden peas and baby lettuces, the sharp, peppery flavor of the arugula, the sweet-and-sour taste of old-fashioned tomato varieties and the delightful colors of edible flowers such as borage and chive. The meltingly smooth flesh of squash, the smooth, shiny skin of the eggplant that varies in color, depending on the variety, from virginal white to midnight blue-black, have something enchanting about them. The colors, shapes, textures, and reflections are a feast for the eyes in the market, long before they are tasted on the plate.

This makes it easy to understand why chefs travel such long distances to buy from Joël, and he sells to them produce of unfailing quality with courtesy and charm. This book is their way of returning his kindnesses. Each of them has taken a vegetable from the annual harvest and used it as the inspiration for a recipe. The result of this combination of love of food and the thirst for knowledge, attention to detail and thorough enjoyment, imagination and practicality, is a selection of recipes that will inspire every reader to seek out and enjoy the best produce in their own neighborhood.

Joël, do you have a favorite season?
"OH, YES!

"WINTER, because that's when I can 'hang up my tools' for just a moment to think about what I did in the previous season, prepare for the next one, look for new plants to grow, and decide what I will need to study and learn for the following year's ventures. This is the time when I think about all the problems and concerns that arose during the previous year's work. But then my love of truck farming gains the upper hand again, so that only the successes of the previous season are what count.

"SPRING, for its first pleasant days, when we plant out the early seedlings and sometimes get the impression that we are in control of what we are doing. For the delight of my customers who have been waiting impatiently for months for those crunchy little radishes, baby carrots, and all the spring vegetables whose flavor is incomparable, such as the baby cauliflowers of April.

"SUMMER, for the ripening of the tomatoes and the fruits that are grown in the tunnels. Such a tremendous amount of expertise is involved in the growing of crops during this period of abundant vegetation, when we need to achieve the impossible: namely, to monitor the development of all the crops at the same time, constantly determining what they need most if they are to grow successfully. It is also the season for meeting new customers in the market, people who love food and who have taken the trouble to travel a long way for our collections of 'fruity vegetables.'

"FALL, because this is the result and the culmination of all the hard work we have been putting in since March, so as to be able to display a wide range of produce on our market carts, for the pleasure of seeing food-lovers who are prepared to stand in line, sometimes for more than half an hour, just for the pleasure of tasting our vegetables."

UNDER THE SKIES
of the
ÎLE-DE-FRANCE

In the nineteenth century, the outer suburbs and small towns that ring Paris, such as Argenteuil, Carrières-sur-Seine, Chatou, Croissy-sur-Seine, Genevilliers, Houilles, or Montesson were nothing more than large villages in the heart of the picturesque landscapes painted by the Impressionists, some of whom lived there. Their farms were the source of fresh produce for the tables of the French capital. The painters have gone, and so have most of the small farms, replaced by factories and housing projects. This has been a great loss for those like Joël Thiébault's family, who once sold their produce in the markets scattered throughout the region.

A kitchen garden in Yerres. Gardeners watering the seedlings, c. 1876–77 by Gustave Caillebotte (1848–1894). Oil on canvas, 35 x 46 in. (90 x 117 cm).

In the fields of Carrières

A string of small settlements line the meanders of the River Seine north-west of Paris. Their names retain the fragrant memory, if not the present reality, of a bygone age: today, their outskirts are part of the urban sprawl of the capital. The fields that once surrounded them have been built over in ever greater density. They have become problem areas and their reputation has suffered. No one would dream of visiting them now for a lazy day by the river.

Joël Thiébault's truck farm is located in Carrières-sur-Seine which, like the other towns mentioned, lies on the right bank of the Seine. Carrières is divided into two parts, reflecting the special topography of the place. There is an upper town, built on a chalk outcrop that overlooks the river, and a lower part, known as La Plaine sur l'Eau (the plain on the water) consisting of a stretch of flat land bordering the river bank. Joël cultivates land in both parts of the town, and it is this diversity of soils and exposures that gives him such great results.

Half his land is located on the limestone hillock originally formed in the Mesozoic era. Most of the soil is chalky and powdery and warms up very quickly in spring, because the land is well drained and exposed to the sun. The rest has a heavier, less permeable consistency, due to the combination of clay and limestone. The limestone is inert, meaning that the action of water does not cause it to break down into calcium carbonate ($CaCO_3$) salts. In soils in which the limestone is active, the $CaCO_3$ is released when it comes into contact with water, making it available for absorption into the root systems of the crops. The presence or absence of calcium carbonate is crucial for plant growth. Some plants cannot tolerate it, but most legumes need it for their growth, so it is important in this instance.

The rest of Joël's land is located in La Plaine sur l'Eau, beside the banks of the Seine. Over the centuries, each time the river has flooded it has deposited alluvial soil, including fine mineral particles that make for a rich, fertile soil that retains water well in high summer, while remaining easy to till in spring when it is sodden. While the powdery soils on the heights have a subsoil consisting of very porous chalk that dries out quickly when the weather becomes warmer in spring, the alluvial soil of the plain is also inclined to "bleach" when dried out by the spring wind. The air temperature is also affected by the microclimate created by the river—milder in winter, cooler in summer. This soil is not too heavy and does not scorch in the sun as do the soils on the higher, exposed ground.

The temperate ocean climate predominates as far inland as the Île-de-France at its western limits. Its action results in milder winters in the Paris Basin, and it attenuates the heat of summer which is generally more oppressive in a city further east such as Strasbourg, which lies on almost the same latitude. The Seine is a navigable waterway, and in order to ensure that ships can sail on it when the water is very high, there are run-offs into which the surplus can be chaneled. These locations are flooded artificially when the river gets too full. La Plaine sur l'Eau is one such run-off area, although it is rarely flooded. The highest water levels occur between January and April; if there is flooding, it is particularly disastrous in the spring, because that's just when many of the seedlings are planted out.

Joël's total spread under cultivation is just 20 hectares (around 50 acres). Many French growers produce four or five times his output. Most in the Île-de-France use the intensive growing methods that are typical of truck farms, which need to produce a constant succession of crops without interruption, so accelerated growth is a requirement. Joël gives his plants space, however, so they are allowed to grow at their own pace.

In the fresh air, away from the nurturing comfort of the tunnels, the plants are at the mercy of the caprices of weather, variations in temperature, and attacks by predators, but all this merely serves to stimulate and strengthen them, enabling them to produce the powerful flavors that are so typical of Joël's produce

That doesn't mean that everything is grown in the open air. Where plants are too delicate, or if they are needed out of season, some sort of protection is needed that will still allow the light to pass through. In the past, this was achieved by using cold frames and greenhouses, but plastic has now replaced glass because it is less fragile, more flexible, and requires much less maintenance. The greenhouses have been turned into "polytunnels," the only way to grow subtropical plants such as tomatoes, eggplant, and melons. This gives them an earlier start and favors the rapid growth which is typical of these plants. The tunnel guarantees them the warmth that they need, even in the summer during cool nights, and protects them in early fall, when the days are not so warm and the nights are often cold.

Summer working conditions inside the tunnels are always extreme. The temperature is always high and the difference between maximum and minimum temperatures is always greater than in the open field. The temperature can rise as high as 122°F (50°C) in high summer, and the ambient humidity merely amplifies the discomfort of the heat. If it isn't too warm, the bees will also be at work. They come from the surrounding hives and take care of the pollination of the melon blossoms. The soil always has to be mulched for summer crops.

Below, left: André, a first-year electronics student, is a part-time but enthusiastic gardener. Below, right: spray-watering young tomato plants before switching to drip-feed irrigation.

The tunnels are planted for twelve months of the year, even thirteen, according to Joël, because sometimes plants from the following crop are inserted among their predecessors; these have to wait for space to be available so that they can grow to full size. Even if space is limited inside the tunnels, that's not because they are small! There are 2 hectares (5 acres) under plastic, a total of 18 tunnels, ranging in length from 50 to 100 feet with volumes of 10,600 to 70,600 cubic feet. The height varies from 8.5 to 11.2 feet.

Joël on his tractor after a hard day's plowing.

The soil, inside and outside the tunnels, is treated, depending on its location. Organic and mineral fertilizers are used and the amount of humus kept constant by adding an organic mixture containing 70 percent humus. Six hectares (about 15 acres) have been zoned for redevelopment, so the crops planted there only receive the bare minimum of feed that they need while ensuring that the humus level remains acceptable. Minimal chemical fertilization is applied to achieve the desired effect. For instance, choosing varieties of vegetables that can be harvested young means that less fertilizer is required than harvesting them when the produce is fully mature. This enables Joël to use the following amounts per hectare (about 2½ acres), taking the crops as a whole: 100 u nitrogen, 66 u phosphate, 205 u potassium and 4 u magnesium—very little for vegetable cultivation.

The farm machinery consists of six tractors ranging in power from 45 hp to 85 hp and various "beasts of burden," such as a root harvester (pay attention, you carrots, turnips, beets, and so on!), a potato windrowing harvester, a bulb windrowing harvester (now it's the turn of the onions...), not forgetting a device for loading and unloading crates on the tractor-trailer and a transporter to take pallets to the warehouse. Chemical herbicides and weed-killer are applied with certain crops and manual weeding may also be necessary.

Joël has a loyal team he can count on. There are nine permanent employees, two of whom have been with him for more than thirty years, and one who has been with him

for around twenty years. Almost everyone else has also been working for him for a long time. Apart from their loyalty, they have something else in common. All are Portuguese and have retained Portuguese nationality, except the youngest, who has taken French nationality. Three or four seasonal workers come and lend a hand at the appropriate times. So the second language spoken on the farm is Portuguese, which Joël understands but claims not to speak as well as he would like.

The workers learn on the job, and all of them are able to multitask, so they can do whatever is necessary. In practice, however, each is employed in whatever he is most skilled at and knowledgeable about. From the start, Joël has had his workers operate in pairs, matching an old-timer with a newcomer so that the younger person absorbs the work culture, but also because new

workers can provide an opportunity for the whole team to learn how to do things differently and put newly acquired knowledge into practice to improve results. Since the farm not only grows vegetables but has to market and sell them as well, part of the team is able to operate wearing two hats. So some people have jobs in both sectors— production and sales—wherever their skills permit. The sellers who you will find working every week at the Thiébault booth in the market often began work on the production side, which explains the ease with which they provide detailed information to customers about a particular item. This in no way diminishes the talents of those who work exclusively in growing the produce.

Saturday morning in the Avenue Président Wilson and it's time for the chefs to do their marketing (left to right: Catherine Guerraz, Taïra Kurihara, Olivier Guyon, Joël, Charlotte Christiansson, and William Ledeuil).

The markets of the sixteenth arrondissement

Joël Thiébault and his team are not content with spending their time out in the fields at Carrières. Wind or rain, snow or shine, four times a week, on Tuesdays, Wednesdays, Fridays, and Saturdays, they load up the truck and drive to Paris to sell their vegetables at the two open-air markets in the fashionable sixteenth arrondissement. They become market traders, pushcart sellers, which is a rather unflattering way of describing what they do. Only a case of force majeure, such as if the Paris stage of the famous Tour de France bicycle race is run over the area usually occupied by the market, could ever interfere with the weekly routine.

So on the fateful days, at around 5:30 A.M., the farm truck heads for the big city. It can be loaded the night before, because the trailer in which the vegetables are transported is refrigerated, ensuring that the produce is absolutely fresh. There are just a few items, such as tomatoes and onion bulbs, that must be loaded on the day itself, because they can be be damaged by chilling.

Only thirty minutes later, the team arrives on site and starts to set up the booth. The weather is an important factor in selling in the open air. The worst kind is an icy spell, because if early morning temperatures drop to 23°F (-5°C), the produce will suffer from frost damage. Rain drives the customers away, but it also has its consolations, because it means the vegetables on the farm, which is only five miles from the Eiffel Tower, will get a good watering.

Joël's customers are just as loyal as his staff, a loyalty inspired by the certainty of finding the greatest variety and quality of vegetables at any time of year, and they are never disappointed

How many people have visited Joël's pushcart since he first started, thirty years ago? There are quite a few of those whom Joël calls his "founding customers." But people move house frequently in the Paris region, more than the French average, and the passage of time leaves its mark. Many customers come from all over Paris, and the luckiest are served by Joël himself, their forebears

having been customers of his grandparents, who used to sell their produce in this neighborhood market; his family has been loyally serving the neighborhood for more than 130 years!

Each year, a growing number of customers buy from Joël in the market, both individuals and food-industry professionals. You can hear a babel of languages, in addition to French. The Portuguese, British, Spanish, Chinese, and many Japanese, Americans, and French-Canadians seek out his booth for the vegetables and herbs they use in their national cuisines, which they have difficulty finding elsewhere. Or perhaps they have read about Joël Thiébault in the national press.

Restaurant owners and caterers have always bought their fresh produce from Joël, the oldest and most faithful of them being Taïra Kurihara (see his recipe on p. 108). More and more of them are becoming regulars. He is always meeting new celebrity chefs, each with their vision of cuisine. Over the years, bonds of friendship have developed between Joël and the chefs who work with his vegetables. He shares with them his profound

Joël, how do you choose your vegetables?

"Discoveries of new varieties may represent the fruits of my research, but may also be inspired by my customers, whether individuals or food and catering professionals. We choose what we grow from the widest possible selection and only after planting a new vegetable, and watching how it develops, its resistance to pests and diseases and, above all, its culinary appeal do I plant it again the following year. The diversity of the range is not just in the variety, we may use a multiplicity of strains or cultivars of the same variety or pick a vegetable at three different stages of its growth. We override all the conventions, customs, and received wisdom when it comes to cropping."

knowledge of what he grows, and each of them shows him, in their own way, the results of their talent. This exchange of ideas has produced all sorts of of experiments. Joël is always thinking of ways in which to improve the flavors and textures of his vegetables, and his customers tell him about vegetables they have discovered on trips abroad. At first, Joël used to deliver to his restaurant customers. When this trade became too big, new customers had to visit the market, because Joël was unable to handle the logistics involved in delivery to so many different addresses.

Everyone, individuals and professionals alike, is listened to with respect. The "old-timers," who have been coming for decades and who sing the praises of Joël's vegetables among their circle of friends or business colleagues, are not necessarily those who are the most dedicated to finding the finest fresh produce; some have discovered Joël through what has been written about him in the press. The enthusiastic neophyte, who might have discovered Joël's vegetables through consuming them in a restaurant dish, or the traveler who has come from a long way away

and who visits the booth as much to taste the vegetables as to see and experience the atmosphere about which he or she has heard so much in the media—all will be served attentively, and every effort will be made to find out what they want and what they expect.

Whatever the customer profile, it is vital to arouse their curiosity. Added to this is the desire to encourage investigation into the pleasures of eating vegetables and, for many, the pleasure of cooking them. Joël and his team are more than keen to share their knowledge to help customers become well acquainted with the vegetables on sale, both in respect of taste and in ways of preparing them, as well as learning about their origins and the importance of preserving the varieties that may be very tasty but whose low yield has condemned them to disappear from the market. Biodiversity maintains a larger gene pool within a given species, enabling a plant to adapt to changes in its environment, as well as providing a wide range of flavors, shapes, and colors to enrich our mealtimes.

Joël, how do you talk about vegetables to your customers?

"We talk to our customers about the origins of the produce—it's one way of making them realize that this interesting vegetable is part of the legacy of nature. We can also explain how biodiversity is achieved by surrounding ourselves with everything that ought to be preserved: if we do not do so, we will have little choice of foods with which to enliven our palates. We show how and why the same vegetable may change texture, flavor, and taste from one week to the next. It is very important to link the life of a vegetable before it is picked with the use that is made of it for the table. We also need to know how to reply to all the questions about the product, knowing that sometimes the purpose of the question is not always just to get an answer, but is a way of testing the depth of our knowledge about vegetables."

Suppose we can't get to the market?

All of the attention paid to the needs of each customer, the shrewd advice, the choice of produce adapted to the season, little-known varieties which, for the reasons mentioned above, deserve to be better known—all this is available at the touch of a button through the Internet or you can get advice by phone, though for that you need to live in or near Paris, so you can join the box scheme. Antoine Meyssonnier and Raimundo Briones, whom Joël met through their regular visits to the market, created the Internet site www.lehautdupanier.com. They are responsible for the delivery every Friday of boxes whose contents are chosen with the greatest care by Joël from the seasonal produce harvested on the Thursday morning. You won't get quite as much background information as you would if you visited the market, but Joël tries to make up for this by writing a blog for the site about the season's produce.

Zucchini blossoms and borage flowers—
an idea suggested by the season to an individual enthusiast.

Carrières-sur-Seine shows the way

From the early Middle Ages, the most powerful abbey in the Île-de-France, the royal abbey of Saint-Denis, owned the land around Carrières; it was called Carrières-Saint-Denis. The abbey built the superb tithe-barn atop the village whose recent, partial restoration gives an idea of what it must have looked like originally. The monks encouraged the land to be cleared

for agriculture, offering protection to craftsmen and merchants whom they attracted to the district.

The main produce of Carrières, which was developed continuously until the ravages of the phylloxera epidemic in 1903, was the grape. The mount on which the village of Carrières stands has a southern exposure and the right type of

pebbly, limestone soil that made it the favorite vineyard of the monks of Saint-Denis. In 1790, the territory of Carrières covered about 1,300 arpents, of which half was planted with vines. An arpent is usually 0.85 of an acre; the measurement fell into disuse after 1840, although local farmers continued to use it to measure their land area, yields, and the cost of leasing land until 1965.

The skies of the Ile-de-France and the reflections of the waters of the Seine are divided into equal thirds at the top and bottom of this painting (facing page) by Claude Monet (1840–1926), who painted the town of Carrières-sur-Seine in 1872. The town was known as Carrières-Saint-Denis until the French Revolution, and intermittently thereafter as well, depending on the vagaries of the relationship between Church and State.

Land reserved for grape-growing was worth far more than arable land.

Joël is a descendant of families of local farmers. They lived here long before the French Revolution, when some of them were given the opportunity to acquire land that had belonged to the abbey. Joël's ancestors grew grapes, cereals, and fruit trees, they reared sheep and cattle, and produced vegetables. Paris, from the late fifteenth century and up to the French Revolution, was one of the most populated cities of Europe and during this period exercised a strong influence over the whole continent. The city experienced a renaissance in the late nineteenth century through the rebuilding of the city by Baron Haussman. The city authorities did all they could to facilitate the supply of agricultural produce from the surrounding area. Without access to modern methods of transportation and food preservation, they were strongly aware of the need to ensure a continuous supply of food for the capital's large population as a guarantee of social harmony.

Carrières-sur-Seine in 2005.

The farmers of Carrières made wine to supply this huge market, as well as producing milk, so they were called "feeders and farmers"

The farmers sold their wine and milk in Paris on a retail basis, delivering it to apartment buildings in the neighborhoods closest to them. From the nineteenth century onward, they extended the service to the wealthiest districts in the capital, from Neuilly to the Eiffel Tower, via the Trocadéro and the Alma, or in what is now the seventeenth arrondissement, as far as the Parc Monceau. They began adding farmyard and garden produce, including fruits and vegetables. They knew what their customers wanted through the almost daily deliveries, so vegetable-growing in Carrières was diversified from the start. Farmers soon began selling produce

in the street markets that opened in the new districts in the west of the city. Joël has kept to the family tradition of being both farmer and market trader. So how long has he himself been selling his produce in the markets? He was an early developer, being only five years old when he discovered market trading. He would practice selling produce in the market at an age when other kids were playing at being firemen. Except that he was playing for real. Behind his little booth, proudly created from two upturned crates, squeezed in next to the booth run by his parents, the little boy would delight customers with his offerings of packets of parsley and sorrel. He still remembers what he charged, which was twenty old francs (about a nickel): that was in 1959.

So in which markets does he sell today? All of them are in the

sixteenth arrondissement of Paris, one on the central reservation of the Avenue du Président Wilson, a handsome tree-lined avenue rendered more impressive by its steep descent. The other in the Rue Gros, a quiet side street where the atmosphere is more intimate. The market in the Avenue du Président Wilson is still known to many as the Alma Market, the name it had prior to 1955 when it was located in the Cours de la Reine, an elegant site close by, which overlooks the Seine, near the Alma Bridge.

This market, where traders and customers have been known to Joël since his childhood as a trader, was the obvious choice when the young man submitted his request for a pitch in the market to the appropriate department of the City of Paris. It was August 1974, and he had just completed his military service. So here he was on October 26 1975, discharged from his military duties and the proud owner of a 4-metre pitch in exactly the same spot he occupies today.

He's made up his mind; he wants to supply varied, adventurous, and delicious produce, with taste and fragrance occupying pride of place

His pitch in the market in the Rue Gros was the choice of a mature and seasoned market trader. In the late 1990s, Joël sold produce in the Nanterre Central Market in the département of Hauts de Seine, where his family had traded since 1962. Confronted with an increasing disparity between the sort of produce he sold and the demand for it, which had once been similar to that of the Avenue du Président Wilson, he had to make a choice. Either he would grow a limited range of vegetables, using the latest production techniques, choosing to produce only what could be mechanically harvested and with a much higher yield, all this to the detriment of flavor, or he could carry on elsewhere in the same way as he was with the produce he was selling in the Alma Market.

Joël reserves a Sunday in September for a reception for chefs at which he shows them his new botanical and food discoveries. Here they are, clockwise from left: Taïra Kurihara, Pascal Barbot, Éric Briffard, and Antoine Meyssonnier.

P. Mikanowski

His choice, to continue growing vegetables that were the result of his researches into tastes and flavors, was rewarded by a favorable commercial climate

At the time, Joël had already begun working with the restaurant owners to whom he delivered, and whose premises were located in the sixteenth and eighth arrondissements. By choosing a site in a market that was both close to his restaurant-owning customers, so he could make deliveries quickly, and one that was frequented by the same sort of customers he served at the Alma Market, he could continue the work he had begun twenty-three years earlier. The market on the Rue Gros met all the requirements, and Joël occupied a pitch there from September 1999, just 100 days before the turn of the millennium— he would say with a wry grin that he hoped he wouldn't meet his Waterloo by the end of the year. Two years later, he was delighted to have gained enough of a loyal following of customers to be able to abandon Nanterre, where he had retained his pitch just in case.

He felt bad to some extent on turning his back on an important episode in the family history. But Joël's attachment to the sixteenth arrondissement is so long-lasting that he feels almost at home there. That's understandable, since the family has been a part of the local scene since the days of the Third Republic (1870–1940).

All vegetables should be treated with respect, from harvest onward.

How to choose vegetables

The tenderness of this freshly picked Swiss chard leaf meant that it was not strong enough to withstand a hailstorm. The flavor and taste are unaffected, however.

HOW TO CHOO
VEGETABLES

Washing under running water. The water pressure will flush out the dirt, sand, insects, and worms.

Wash them in several changes of water (at least three). Vegetables should be carefully rubbed and mixed, then transferred by hand to another sink or bowl containing clean, cold water.

How to wash vegetables

Raw vegetables and fresh herbs can be stored for longer periods by improving their microbiological properties. This is achieved simply by first immersing them in water containing a very small amount of bleach (2 drops of bleach per 2½ cups [1 pint] water) then rinsing them in fresh water and draining them.

P. Mikanowski

Once washed, rinsed, and drained, fresh herbs should be laid on absorbent paper, rolled in it, then stored in a hermetically sealed container in the refrigerator.

SE AND STORE AND HERBS

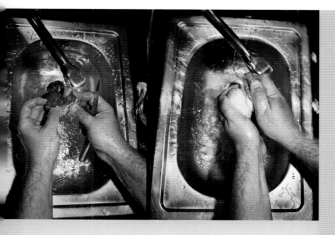

Useful information

All vegetables need to be washed thoroughly, including onions, garlic, shallots, and fresh herbs, because in addition to insects, they may contain the eggs of parasitic worms, their chrysalises or larvae, traces of chemicals used in modern farming, or traces of organic compost based on fecal matter.

Never soak any vegetables or fresh herbs except potatoes in water, because not only does long soaking encourages the growth of bacteria, it causes significant loss of minerals and vitamins.

The wrong way:

Never drain vegetables by turning the bowl upside down, because the sand or dirt will remain in the bottom.

To help tomatoes ripen, remove the stalks and turn them stem end downward.

PASSIONATE ABO

UT VEGETABLES

SAMOS
SPINACH

by Joël

Samos spinach The Persians considered spinach to be the prince of vegetables. The plant originates from northern India and reached Europe via Moorish Spain; it spread rapidly and soon supplanted the rather flavorless common orache that had been cultivated hitherto. Today, the range of spinach varieties makes it possible to grow the plant all year round in France, except when the weather is particularly cold and destroys the roots, or in hot spells when it grows too fast and dies back. My favorite variety is Samos spinach, an heirloom French variety produced by the firm Clause that I pick from around March 10 through April 8. Perhaps I like it so much because it is at its best in early spring when the earth is coming back to life, or because of the handsome drapery of the leaves on the stem, an appearance that the newer varieties lack. I certainly prefer it for the memory of the delicate texture of its young shoots—eaten in a salad or quickly sautéed with a nut of butter—which I always find mouth-watering. I imagine that you might feel the same about spinach when you see and read the recipe that FRANÇOIS BROUILLY has created for this book, revealing his talent as an "enlightened amateur" cook—a worthy successor to his father, Jean, owner of the restaurant Tarare.

SAMOS

by François Brouilly

SPINACH

1

Bring a pan of water to the boil and sprinkle in a few drops of vinegar. Add the eggs and boil for 4 minutes. Stop the cooking by putting the eggs in cold water. Shell them under a thin stream of running water. Reserve.

2

Peel the celery root and cut into thick strips, as for French fries. Combine 1 cup (250ml) water with the milk and season with salt and the saffron. Pour this into a saucepan and add the celery root fingers. Bring to the boil and cook until the celery root is done but still firm, about 12 minutes. Remove from the heat and leave to infuse.

3

Top and tail the spinach and wash thoroughly in several changes of water. Drain well before cooking in melted butter in a sauté pan or large wok. Stir constantly with a spatula and a garlic clove impaled on the tines of a fork. Season with salt and pepper. The spinach is cooked as soon as it has wilted and the texture and color have changed. Drain the cooked spinach and reserve it.

4

To serve, make a nest of spinach on each serving dish and carefully place a whole cooked egg in the center of each nest. Slice the egg open at table so that the yolk runs out over the spinach in front of each diner. Serve immediately, accompanied by the celery root fingers and sprinkled with chive flowers.

Recommended wine: White Beaujolais, Chardonnay Pinot Gris 2003.

Serves 4

A few drops vinegar
4 medium eggs
1 celery root
1 cup (250 ml) milk
Salt and pepper
1 pinch powdered saffron
8 cups (1 kg) Samos spinach
About ½ cup (125 g) butter
1 garlic clove
20 chive flowers

A scoop of
SAMOS
SPINACH,
with soft-boiled
egg & celery
root fingers

KELVEDON WONDER
FRENCH GARDEN PEA

by Joël

Kelvedon Wonder pea The French garden pea experienced its glory days at Versailles during the reign of Louis XIV, and it appears to have spread throughout Europe, enjoying the same success. New English and Dutch varieties emerged in the seventeenth century, thanks to the hard work of the growers of the period who carefully selected the right varieties and practiced diversification. After 1800, varieties such as Marly and Clamart appeared in the Île-de-France, but it was in the next century that the production of fresh garden peas exceeded that of dried peas. Kelvedon Wonder—a variety I chose to promote a few years ago—is of English origin, as the name suggests. The seed is wrinkled when ready for sowing, and it is richer in sugar and lower in starch than smooth-skinned peas such as the Douce Provence. Although it is less frost-resistant and does not ripen as early as French varieties, Kelvedon Wonder does not turn floury as soon as a ray of sunshine warms it. Yet, however good the variety, the presentation is also crucial if it is to whet the gourmet's appetite. I try to use young, tender pods—8 ounces (250 g) of peas per 2¼ pounds (1 kg) of pods. They melt in the mouth and are a meal in themselves. In fact, many of my friends tell me that they eat them raw. Others love them so much they start eating them on their way home from my booth, and I often wonder if they save any for the diners at their restaurants!

The green pea is an exceptional vegetable for its sweet and subtle flavor and the fleeting tenderness of its flesh. It was praised by the Sun King and inspires the creativity of the true artists who are today's chefs. So it was natural for me to offer this rare pearl from the garden to JEAN-FRANÇOIS PIÈGE, chef of the famous restaurant LES AMBASSADEURS, which forms part of the Hotel de Crillon. PIÈGE is a cunning alchemist who combines modernity with tradition, and I was curious to see what he would come up with.

KELVEDON WONDER

by Jean-François Piège

FRENCH GARDEN PEA

Creamy French-style Pea Soup

1
For the soup

Bring the chicken broth to the boil. Remove from the heat, infuse the garden peas in their pods in the liquid for 20 minutes, then filter through a conical sieve, reserving the liquid.

Shell the peas and sauté them in a little olive oil. Bring the chicken broth back to the boil and pour it over the peas, add the butter and the sugar and bring back to the boil for a few minutes. Season and add the mint leaves.

Transfer the mixture to a blender and reduce to a smooth liquid. Then strain through a fine hair sieve and cool as quickly as possible.

2
Royale

Heat the milk to 150°F (65°C), then combine with the foie gras in a food processor. Add the eggs one at a time. Season the mixture and push it through a cheesecloth. Leave it in the refrigerator for at least 3 hours. Skim off any foam with a skimmer. Butter individual molds with softened butter. Fill the molds half-full of the mixture and cook them in a fan-assisted oven at 180°F (80°C) for 1 hour 10 minutes. Remove from the oven and leave to rest for 20 minutes before serving.

3
Emulsion

Combine all the ingredients for the emulsion in a sauté pan, then cook to a temperature of 130°F (55°C). Check the seasoning and strain through a conical sieve into a large bowl. Then beat with an electric whisk until it is frothy throughout, making it into a mousse.

4
Garnish and presentation

Arrange the garnish on the Royale, pour the pea soup round it and top with the emulsion.

French-style Peas

1

Shell the peas, separating the small ones from the large.

2

Make a purée by cooking the larger peas in a teaspoon of olive oil, then add the hot chicken stock—reserving a few tablespoons—and boil for 3 minutes. Pour into a blender and reduce to a smooth purée, then strain the mixture through a fine hair sieve. There should be about 2 tablespoons of purée.

3
Finish and presentation

In a cast-iron pot, heat a teaspoon of the olive oil and add the country ham. Cook for a few moments, then remove the ham. Add the butter to the pot and when it has melted add the smaller peas, cooking for a few moments on low heat. Then add the reserved chicken broth and cook for 5 minutes.

Add the lettuce leaves, reduce the liquid and combine it with the pea purée and the rest of the olive oil. Add the veal broth and black pepper.

Garden Pea Ice Cream

1

Combine all the ingredients in a blender, then put them into a Pacojet or other ice-cream maker and stir until ready.

2

Shape into balls with a scoop and serve in a cocktail glass. Sprinkle with the bacon bits.

Recommended wine: Hermitage Blanc 1999, Jean-Louis Chave.

Serves 4

Creamy French-style Pea Soup

For the soup
1⅓ cups (350 ml) chicken broth
8 oz (250 g) Kelvedon Wonder peas
1 scant cup (200 ml) olive oil
¼ cup (50 g) butter
2 teaspoons (10 g) sugar
⅛ teaspoon (2 g) salt
3 mint leaves

Royale
1¼ cups smoked milk
14 oz (400 g) foie gras
8 medium eggs
Butter for greasing

Emulsion
2½ tablespoons (40ml) olive oil
1 teaspoon (4 g) salt
1 teaspoon (4 g) sugar
1¾ cups (400 g) Kelvedon Wonder peas
1¼ cups (300 ml) light cream
25 mint leaves

Garnish
20 butterhead lettuce leaves
20 slices of Spanish pancetta
Cooked dried peas
Finely sliced peppermint leaves

French-style Peas
1 scant cup (200 g) Kelvedon Wonder peas
3 teaspoons (10 ml) olive oil
2½ cups (600 ml) white chicken stock
4 slices country ham
¼ cup (50 g) butter
20 butterhead lettuce leaves
¼ cup (50 ml) veal broth
Freshly ground black pepper

Garden Pea Ice Cream
1 scant cup (200 g) Kelvedon Wonder peas
1 scant cup (200 g) pea pods
3 teaspoons (14 g) sugar
2 teaspoons (10 g) table salt
1¾ cups (400 ml) milk
1¾ cups (400 ml) chicken broth
3 tablespoons (70 ml) olive oil
4 egg yolks
1 teaspoon (5 g) stabilizer (Cremodan)
4 butterhead lettuce leaves
Bacon bit sprinkles

Variations in taste and texture in KELVEDON WONDER GARDEN PEAS, French-style

SPRING FLORENCE FENNEL

by Joël

Spring Florence fennel When I visit one of my polytunnels at the end of a hot June day and the strongly aromatic fragrance of aniseed hits my nose, I am immediately transported in my mind to the dry, stony paths of the south of France. But the reality before my eyes is just as attractive; the fragrance is that of the fennel bulbs, which I normally plant in mid-March so as to protect them from the last winter frosts. In the first row of plants, I can clearly see the flattened bulbs, from which grow long stems topped by elegant feathery green leaves; green, although sometimes slightly bronzed, a hint of the relationship between our cultivated fennel and its wild cousin that still grows along the roadside. In summer, this Mediterranean plant grows well in the Paris region, and we offer our customers bunches of three or four bulbs, ensuring they retain all of their foliage. When conditions are right, a root that has remained in the soil may also produce two baby fennel plants, which we then pick in their miniature form, to the delight of Parisian connoisseurs.

So, I naturally asked someone from the south to cook this vegetable. But her south is the Deep South—far away and across the ocean—because she comes from Argentina. RAQUEL CARENA is a brilliant cook and, moreover, she is self-taught. She knows how to extract all the subtleties from the aniseed-flavored bulb in order for it to grace our tables. Some fortunate people will have had the opportunity to hear her talk about the fresh market cuisine that she practices daily at LE BARATIN, her restaurant and wine bar in Belleville, along with PINOUCHE, a sommelier without the title but an acknowledged wine expert nevertheless.

SPRING FLORENCE FENNEL

by Raquel Carena

Serves 4

1 head new garlic
2¼ lb (1 kg) spring Florence fennel bulbs
2 tablespoons (30 g) blanched almonds
⅓ cup (100ml) olive oil
2 oz (30 g) yellow raisins, 6–7 coriander seeds
1 untreated orange, 1 pinch saffron strands
Salt and pepper
1 bunch fresh coriander (cilantro)

1

Slice the garlic lengthwise into petals. Do the same with the fennel.

2

Arrange the almonds on a cookie sheet and bake in a preheated 180 °C (350°F) oven for a few minutes until they turn golden. Transfer them to a mortar and crush them.

3

In a cast-iron casserole, heat 2 tablespoons (30 ml) olive oil. Add the garlic and fennel and cook, stirring constantly for 5 minutes. Add the yellow raisins, crushed almonds, and coriander seeds. Zest the orange peel finely with a zester and add it to the mixture with the saffron.
Season with salt and pepper.
Simmer on low heat for about 10 minutes, then add the juice from the orange and the rest of the oil.

4

Stop the cooking when the fennel is cooked but still "al dente" (crunchy). Leave it to cool until cold. Chop the fresh coriander and sprinkle it over the dish. Serve cold.

This dish can be made in advance and will keep in the refrigerator for four days.

Recommended wine: Tavel Blanc 2004, Cuvée Sel d'Argent, from Eric Pfifferling.

Escabeche of SPRING FLORENCE FENNEL **with orange**

BALTIMORE
CAULIFLOWER

by Joël

Baltimore cauliflower

One of the earliest spring vegetables ... and the first edible flower! As soon as they glimpse the first signs of good weather ahead, the "leaf" cabbages raise their heads, drinking in the cool dew of early March. The burgeoning leaves turn to the light as the days grow longer and the air temperature begins to increase during the day, accelerating the growth of the plant. But, luckily for the consumer, the nights are often chilly at this time of year and put stress on the young adult plant. The result soon makes itself apparent: like most of the plants in our regions, the cabbage immediately seeks to ensure its continuity, so it can be said that the cold nights initiate the flowering. It is at this precise, very brief moment that I hurry to pick the budding flower. Taking every precaution, due to its fragility, it will be delivered the very next day to JAMIN, and I shall be reassured and certain that my produce will be used to its best advantage by BENOÎT GUICHARD, chef and owner of this restaurant. This nature-lover, with the culinary talent that has made him famous, will permit a final "flowering" on the plate by combining produce from the soil with that from the sea.

BALTIMORE
by Benoît Guichard
CAULIFLOWER

1
Crawfish jello

Crush the 16 crawfish heads in 5 tablespoons (40 ml) olive oil. Mince the onion and shallots and cook in a cast-iron casserole in the remaining 5 tablespoons (40 ml) olive oil until slightly colored. Add to the crushed crawfish mixture. Slice the tomato in half and add it with the tomato paste and star anise. Add 4 cups (1 liter) water, the bouquet garni, a dash of salt, and 3 turns of the peppermill. Cook at a very slow boil for 30 minutes.
Soak the unflavored gelatin leaves in cold water. Strain the crawfish mixture in a conical sieve, then degrease it well. Add the softened gelatin leaves, then strain again. Reserve the mixture.

2
Cauliflower cream

Slice the cauliflower and blanch it in boiling salted water for 2 to 3 minutes. Rinse under cold water and drain well. Heat the chicken broth and when boiling add the cauliflower. Add a pinch of curry powder, cover, and simmer for 10 minutes. Strain, reserving the liquid, and press the cauliflower through a potato ricer back into the liquid. Reduce the liquid to half by boiling it uncovered. Combine the cornstarch with 4 tablespoons of water. Add this mixture to the broth and beat with a whisk until it boils, then cook for 3 minutes. In a small bowl, combine the egg yolk, light cream, and heavy cream. Add this mixture to the soup, beating constantly, and remove from the heat as soon as it comes to the boil. Transfer the mixture to a blender, process, then strain through a conical sieve. Check the seasoning. Chill.

Serves 4

Crawfish jello
16 crawfish
(16 crawfish heads, tails reserved for garnish)
10 tablespoons (80 ml) olive oil
1 onion
2 shallots
1 small tomato, skinned
1 tablespoon tomato paste
1 star anise
1 small bouquet garni
Salt and pepper
4 unflavored gelatin leaves
Water for soaking

Cauliflower cream
1 lb 12 oz (800 g) white cauliflower
2½ cups (600 ml) chicken broth
1 pinch curry powder
2 tablespoons (30 g) cornstarch
⅓ cup (100 ml) light cream
5 teaspoons (50 ml) heavy cream
1 egg yolk

Garnish
1¾ oz (50 g) celery sticks
4 baby red radishes
2½ oz (70 g) carrots
2¼ oz (60 g) cucumber
1 scant cup (200 ml) olive oil
2 sprigs chervil

Crawfish jello in cream of WHITE CAULIFLOWER

3
Garnish
Cut the celery, radishes, carrots, and cucumber into ¼-inch (5-mm) dice. Blanch the celery, radishes, and carrots in boiling salted water for a few moments, then mix with the raw cucumber. Shell the crawfish tails. Heat 1 scant cup (200 ml) olive oil in a sauté pan until very hot and lightly sauté the crawfish until they are cooked through and slightly colored.

4
Finishing and assembling
Warm the jello slightly to soften it. Take four soup bowls and distribute the diced vegetable mixture between them. Pour ⅓ cup (100 ml) of the softened jello into each bowl and place in the refrigerator. Pour 5 teaspoons (50 ml) of the cauliflower cream on top of the set jello, then add 4 crawfish tails to each bowl and decorate with chervil.

Recommended wine: Savennières 2002.

YOUNG CARROT

by Joël

Young carrots

Young carrots If one had to name a universal vegetable par excellence, the carrot would certainly be in the running, being grown all over the world in every type of climate. It seems to have originated in two places simultaneously, since there are two distinct types: an Oriental type whose roots range in color from purple to yellow—and which is still found predominantly in Asia—and a Western type whose roots, ranging in color from white to yellow, have evolved into orange. The latter is by far the most frequently found variety. It is a great pity for Western gourmets that none of the red Japanese or Indian carrot varieties are included in the official seed catalogs of Europe. We could rightly view this as an attack on our freedom to choose what we eat, because these carrot varieties could easily be grown over here. This control over our seed heritage tends to favor the disappearance of less popular varieties. Yet, although they may not be as prolific as the commonest kinds, they often have the best and most interesting flavors. In the case of carrots, these varieties would also have the advantage of brightening up our dreary and monotonous vegetable dishes. So, the truck farmers who grow their produce near big cities in order to supply the metropolises should put their know-how and imagination to good use and grow something *other* than the same old carrot that can be found on any supermarket shelf.

Freshness is essential, especially at the start of the harvest when we pull up those beautiful and slim orange, yellow, white, or violet roots that are just about the diameter of a thick pencil. They are delicate and fragile; tender because they are immature, fragrant because they are fresh, and tasty because they have not been forced. These princesses of the garden could not have done better than to find PASCAL BARBOT, chef at L'ASTRANCE, who has worked with his front-of-house partner CHRISTOPHE ROHAT to make their restaurant one of the most promising in Paris, where tables are highly sought after. His shining creativity is matched by his modesty when complimented and thanked by the restaurant's patrons. These young carrots may be lilliputians in the world of root vegetables, but they soon turn into giants when cooked by Pascal Barbot.

YOUNG CARROT
by Pascal Barbot

Serves 4

1 bunch young carrots, washed but unpeeled
Sea salt
Olive oil
Norway spruce shoots or dillweed

Carotene butter
½ bunch young carrots
4 teaspoons (20 g) butter
1 teaspoon orange-flower water

Carrot-cake sauce
2 tablespoons (60 g) sugar
4 tablespoons (60 g) all-purpose flour
1 teaspoon baking soda
1 teaspoon cinnamon
Coarse salt
3 tablespoons (50 ml) peanut oil
⅔ cup (150 g) grated young carrots
2 whole eggs

1
Cook the bunch of unpeeled carrots in a large saucepan of boiling salted water for 3 minutes. Rinse in iced water. Scrape the carrots lightly with a knife and season at the last minute with sea salt and olive oil. Garnish with young Norway spruce shoots or dillweed.

2
Carotene butter
Put the half bunch of carrots through a juicer and bring the juice to the boil. Filter it, keeping only the orange particles (carotene). Blend them with the butter and orange-flower water.

3
Carrot-cake sauce
Combine all the ingredients except the eggs in a blender. Process, adding the eggs one by one. Heat the carrot-cake sauce in a saucepan and simmer for 20 minutes, stirring frequently. Strain through a conical sieve.

4
On a warmed plate, arrange the seasoned carrots, the carrot-cake sauce, and the carotene butter. Serve immediately.

Recommended wine: Montlouis-sur-Loire 2003, Brut non dosé, Jacky Blot.

YOUNG CARROTS, carotene butter, and carrot-cake sauce

CHIVE FLOWER
by Joël

Chive flowers

What's happening in the garden? For several days now, regular rows of stiff stalks have replaced the fragile, bunched shoots of chives. They poked their noses above ground during the first fine days after the long winter sleep. Those that were the palest green seemed to have difficulty in returning to life. But eventually they won through and became such elegant "fine herbs" that we decided to cut them a first time. Still they persevered and bravely put forth new, velvety shoots that pointed toward the skies. This time, however, they swore that they would not be captured again and, one after the other, their heads swelled, forming lines of plumed helmets, like those of the Spanish conquistadors. They did not count on the gourmet, who lay in wait for them, eager to cut off those still-enclosed buds to give pleasure to his friends. There is no more salvation for those plants that have succeeded in flowering, showing off their pretty pink balls of petals, because they too will be used to flavor and enrich a number of dishes. FRÉDÉRIC ANTON, chef of the restaurant PRÉ CATELAN in Paris, strikes that curious balance between meticulous rigor and epicurean delight and deftly demonstrates here why chive flowers are sometimes called "appetite tails."

CHIVE FLOWER
by Frédéric Anton

1

Bring the vinegar to the boil, cool, then refrigerate it.

2

In a preserving jar (Mason jar), arrange layers of the flowers, interspersed with the birdseye chili peppers, garlic, pearl or pickling onions, coarse salt, bay leaves, thyme, coriander seeds, black peppercorns, and tarragon. Continue layering until the jar is filled.

3

Cover the contents of the jar with the vinegar. Close the jar, ensuring the rubber seal is properly in place, and leave upside down in the refrigerator for two months before using.

To make 2½ cups (1 l)

2 cups (500 ml) white wine vinegar
10½ oz (300 g) chive flowers (buds)
8 red birdseye chili peppers
8 green birdseye chili peppers
4 new garlic cloves
4 pearl or pickling onions
1 teaspoon (5 g) coarse (kosher) salt
3 bay leaves
2 sprigs thyme
1 teaspoon coriander seeds
1 teaspoon black peppercorns
1 sprig tarragon

CHIVE
FLOWERS,
pickled in vinegar

by Joël

AZUR STAR
KOHLRABI

Azur Star kohlrabi What a weird plant! It looks like a sort of Cavalier cabbage, a cabbage on a long, tree-like stalk that can grow to more than six feet (two meters) high. But there's a surprise: when examined closely, you'll find the leaves of this cabbage are firmly attached to a fleshy ball that may vary in color from greenish-white through violet. You might think this is a weird kind of turnip with cabbage leaves (and another name for kohlrabi is indeed "turnip cabbage"), but if you look more closely, the "turnip" is not a root at all but a swelling resulting from the hypertrophy—overgrowth—of the stem. The plant's real root is long and narrow and runs deep into the soil, as it should. If you take the risk and bite into this distorted stem, you will find its flesh crunchy and juicy but quite tender. This vegetable—or, to be more precise, its Azur Star variety—is the one that ALAIN PÉGOURET, chef at the restaurant LE LAURENT, has chosen to work with. Thanks to his enthusiasm and burgeoning creativity, combined with his precision, he will reveal just what is so good about this ... ball of cabbage.

AZUR STAR
KOHLRABI
by Alain Pégouret

Serves 4

Kohlrabi sauce
2¼ lb (1 kg) Azur Star kohlrabi
Salt
⅖ cup (100 ml) broth made with aromatic flowers
⅖ cup (100ml) olive oil

Light cream emulsion
1 lb 5 oz (600 g) Azur Star kohlrabi
⅖ cup (100 ml) grapeseed oil
2 teaspoons (10 g) finely chopped kohlrabi
with mixed vegetables, cooked to a purée
¼ teaspoon (2 g) grated lime zest
1 scant cup (200 ml) whipped cream

Jumbo shrimp
20 jumbo shrimp
7 cups (2 l) broth made with coriander (cilantro)
flowers, chive flowers and stems,
grated lemon and orange zest

To finish
Salt & mignonnette pepper
A few tablespoons vinaigrette dressing
Coriander flowers
Chive flowers

1
Kohlrabi sauce
Wash and peel the kohlrabi, cut into large cubes, then cook in a saucepan of boiling water, adding salt at the end of the cooking time. Rinse, drain, and carefully dry with kitchen paper. Put in the bowl of a food processor and combine with the aromatic flower broth and the olive oil to obtain a smooth sauce. Rectify the seasoning and reserve.

2
Light cream emulsion
Wash the kohlrabi and cut into ¼-inch (0.5-cm) dice.
Heat the grapeseed oil in a saucepan. Add the chopped kohlrabi and season to taste. Cook gently, stirring regularly so that the mixture does not color. Cover and simmer for 10 to 15 minutes. At the end of this time, remove the lid and allow all the vegetable liquid to evaporate. Push the dry vegetables through a sieve. Mix this purée with the finely chopped kohlrabi and vegetable mixture, grated lime zest, and whipped cream. Refrigerate until required.

3
Jumbo shrimp
Cook the jumbo shrimp in the broth for 3 minutes. Shell the shrimp tails and reserve them.

4
Assembling the dish
Divide the kohlrabi sauce between 6 shallow bowls. Use a soupspoon to fashion a large quenelle of the light cream emulsion and place it in the center of each bowl. Season the shrimp, sprinkle a little vinaigrette dressing over them and arrange them around the quenelles. Sprinkle with a few coriander flowers and chive flowers.

Recommended wine: Viognier, Condrieux 2003.

AZUR STAR KOHLRABI **sauce with a light cream and lime zest emulsion
and aromatic jumbo shrimp**

MUSSELBURGH
LEEKS

by Joël

The Musselburgh Leek

Its origins may be uncertain, but the leek has been cultivated for centuries in the Mediterranean basin, where it was the supreme reward granted by the great Pharaoh Khufu to his bravest warriors. It was also a delicacy fit for the Roman Emperor Nero, who ate huge quantities, believing it would improve his voice. The Welsh, in their battles with the Ancient Britons, used the leek as a sign of recognition and decided to make it their emblem. In those days, the plant did not have the same characteristics as it has today; it was not until the sixteenth century that the long shaft of the leek, which emerges quite early in the year, could be grown alongside the shorter shaft that is very cold-resistant. Today, the main leek-growing countries in Europe are France and Belgium. The technique used by the Belgians consists in planting the seedlings in a hole about 1 inch (2.5 cm) in diameter and 10 inches (25 cm) deep. This means that the shoots have a long white section of stem at the root, but can also lead to a standardization of flavors that should characterize each variety. To avoid this problem, I use the traditional method employed for centuries by the truck farmers and growers on the outskirts of the cities, but with the help of as many mechanical aids as I can muster. The leeks are planted mechanically, buried up to 4 inches (10 cm) deep. They develop this way and are then mulched when they have grown tall enough. Mulching, in this case, means shoring the soil up around them to blanch the stem. This method produces plants that are not so "stringy" at the end of winter. As long as there have not been long periods when growth has stopped altogether due to the cold, the mild flavor and melting flesh of our vegetable will be a delight. LOUIS-JACQUES VANNUCCI, owner of the restaurant SOLEIL in Saint-Ouen, a suburb of Paris, and his chef, FRÉDÉRIC THÉVENET, show us how the "poor man's asparagus" can become a king of the table.

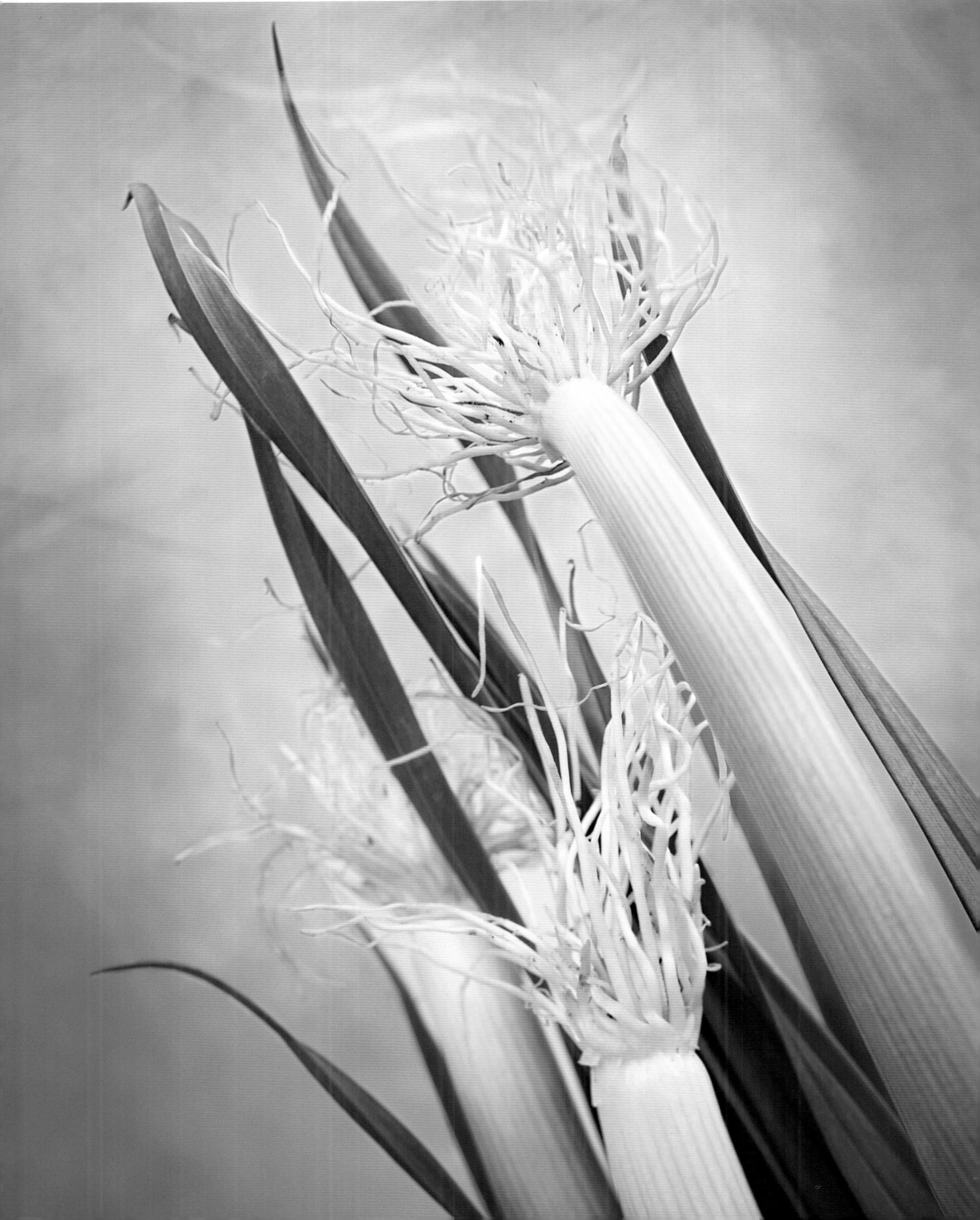

MUSSELBURGH LEEKS
by Louis-Jacques Vannucci & Frédéric Thévene

Serves 4

Sealing paste
4 cups (500 g) all-purpose flour
2½ cups (600 ml) water
⅓ cup (80 g) coarse (kosher) salt

24 Musselburgh leeks
1 large handful (about 4 oz/125 g) fresh hay
1 scant cup (200 ml) Chenin Blanc wine
1 pinch sugar
1 tablespoon water
4 x 1-oz (30-g) slices of cooked country ham
Sea salt and freshly ground white pepper
¼ cup (50 g) unsalted butter
Olive oil
2 teaspoons butter
1 shallot
3 Belles de Fontenay potatoes or other waxy salad potatoes
1 scant cup (200 ml) chicken broth
2 lovage leaves
Sea salt and freshly ground white pepper
6 almonds, blanched and slivered
1 bunch chives with flowers
Sherry vinegar and olive oil

1
Sealing paste
Combine all the ingredients in order to obtain a smooth, thick paste.

2
Leeks
Clean the leeks and trim them, keeping ¾ inch (2 cm) of green on the white stem and reserving the green leek tops. Cook the stems for 2 minutes in boiling salted water, then rinse in iced water. Rinse the hay in water. Drain it well and put it into a large saucepan. Add the Chenin Blanc wine, a pinch of sugar, and 1 tablespoon of water. Bring to the boil, remove from the heat, cover, and leave to infuse for 20 minutes.

3
Drain the hay and cover the bottom of a casserole with it. Arrange the leeks in tight layers over the hay. Cover with the country ham and season with salt and pepper. Add butter and olive oil. Seal the lid on the casserole with the sealing paste, place in a preheated 450°F (230°C) oven and bake for 20 minutes.

4
Cream of lovage
Melt a little butter in a frying pan. Chop the shallot coarsely. Reserve a little for the vinaigrette, and fry the rest until it is transparent. Add 2 oz (50 g) of potato and moisten with the chicken broth. When the potato is almost cooked through, add the green parts of the leeks and the lovage leaves. Season with salt and pepper. Cook for another 2 minutes. Process in a food processor and put on ice immediately.

5
Potato salad with chive flowers
Slice two potatoes into matchstick strips. Blanch them in boiling, salted water just until they are crunchy, about 5 minutes. Drain and put on ice. Slice the almonds into slivers, trim and wash the chive flowers, and chop the chives finely. In a large bowl, make a vinaigrette dressing with a little sherry vinegar, salt and pepper, the reserved minced shallot,

Little MUSSELBURGH LEEKS with country ham cooked in hay, cream of lovage, and potato salad with chive flowers

and a tablespoon of olive oil. Add the matchstick potatoes to the dressing and sprinkle with the chopped chives.

6
Assembling the dish
On a large flat serving dish, place a tablespoon of the chilled cream of lovage. On top, arrange six warm leeks side by side, with the warm

country ham crosswise over the last leek in the row. At the side of the plate, make a little pile of the potato salad and sprinkle with chive petals, sea salt crystals, and slivered almonds. Serve immediately.

Recommended wine: Savennières, Domaine des Beaumard, Cuvée Saint-Yves 2000.

RED RHUBARB

by Joël

Red Rhubarb

Rhubarb is a greatly undervalued vegetable. Cultivated by growers in the Paris region since the nineteenth century, rhubarb arrived from China and Mongolia. This sturdy plant may survive for more than twenty years on the same plot of land. Its emergence marks the spring awakening of vegetation and the end of the winter lethargy that overcomes most perennials such as sorrel, globe artichokes, and cardoons. The little bud soon opens to reveal a soft, crinkly leaf, with a stalk that quickly elongates into a long stem. The plant grows tall and smothers the small herbaceous plants that dare to sprout too close to it. We harvest it in late March as the stems thicken, being careful to remove the flower stalks before the flower can develop. We produce two varieties of rhubarb: the red variety grows earliest, but the other, gray-stemmed variety is more resistant to the early heat waves. The differences in color between stalks of the same variety does not—contrary to what many consumers believe—indicate that the red stalks have a higher sugar content, or even that they mature better. I have been proving this for many years by picking the pale-colored stems as early as possible, at which point they have a wonderful flavor. The belief that a red color indicates sweetness is so deeply ingrained in some people's minds that they sometimes buy bunches of beet tops and try to use them for making desserts! I am fond of the combination of sweetness and sourness that is present in this vegetable. My whole family enjoys rhubarb, which can be combined with fish or meat but is more frequently made into a dessert. It is not unusual to find FRANÇOISE, my wife, helped by our two daughters, PAULINE and AMANDINE, creating a homemade dessert recipe to delight the whole family.

RED RHUBARB
by Françoise Thiébault

Rhubarb Tart

1

The day before, cut the rhubarb into short 1-inch (2-cm) lengths. Put a piece of ginger root in a press to obtain about 1 teaspoon of liquid. Mix both together with 2 tablespoons (50 g) of the sugar and leave overnight.

2

Shortcrust dough

The following day, combine the sugar, butter, and salt until smooth and fluffy, then gradually beat in the flour. Fill a tart pan with the mixture, pushing it outward and into place with the palm of your hand.

3

To finish the filling, whip the crème fraîche in a bowl with the remaining ¼ cup (75 g) sugar, then add the flour, a whole egg, and an egg yolk. The mixture should be smooth. Drain the lengths of rhubarb and fold them into the cream, then spread the mixture in the bottom of the tart pan. Bake the tart in a preheated 450°F (240°C) oven for 45 minutes.

Strawberry Compote

1

Wash and hull the strawberries. Drain in a colander then put in a bowl with the sugar and leave to rest for 1 hour.

2

Soak the gelatin leaves in cold water. Cook the sugared strawberries for just a few minutes on low heat. Dissolve the gelatin in the mixture while it is still warm. Divide the mixture between 8 ramekins. Leave to cool, then refrigerate until chilled.

Recommended wine: Vouvray Moelleux Huet 2002.

Serves

Shortcrust dough
⅓ cup (100 g) sugar
1 scant cup (200 g) butter
1 pinch salt
2½ cups (300 g) all-purpose flour

Filling
2 lb (900 g) rhubarb
1 teaspoon ginger juice, made from ginger root
½ cup (125 g) sugar
2 tablespoons crème fraîche
3 tablespoons all-purpose flour
1 whole egg and 1 egg yolk

Strawberry compote
3½ cups (800 g) strawberries
1½ oz (40 g) sugar
6 leaves unflavored gelatin

RHUBARB
**tart with
strawberry compote**

BEEFHEART

by Joël

SPRING CABBAGE

Beefheart spring cabbage Cabbage was known as *krambé* in Ancient Greece and according to mythology, it was considered worthy of being served to Zeus, king of the gods. Its European origins make it one of the earliest vegetables known to Western civilization.

The Beefheart cabbage has a firm, pointed shape. In French it is also known as *cabus*, from the Latin *caput*, meaning "head." It is of the type known as Easter cabbage, of which there are several varieties of cultivar adapted to local French growing conditions, such as Très Hâtif d'Étampes, Précoce de Louviers, Pointu de Châteaurenard, and Cœur de Bœuf des Vertus. This cabbage is another harbinger of spring, sprouting in early April under cold frames. It is the definitive sign that winter has ended as far as our seasonal dishes are concerned. The first cabbage harvest reveals a delicate, pale green heart surrounded by large, tender leaves that are still crunchy and firm due to their rapid growth. The warm weather of May gives the cabbage its volume; the head becomes firmer, and when mature it will have that delicious flavor and crunchy texture so characteristic of this variety of spring cabbage.

The Beefheart spring cabbage could only have been given to JEAN-LOUIS NOMICOS—one of the most generous chefs of his generation and owner of the restaurant LASSERRE—so that he could weave his magic. We are well aware of his sensitivity and creativity, yet he still manages to surprise us by producing a very special and personal creation.

BEEFHEART
by Jean-Louis Nomicos
SPRING CABBAGE

Serves 4

1 beefheart spring cabbage
1 lobe duck foie gras
1 thick slice (14 oz/400 g) red tuna
Sea salt and peppercorns
8 small new onions
1 oz (25 g) fresh ginger root, thinly sliced
⅓ cup (100 ml) Montegottero lemon vinegar
1 sprig coriander flowers, to garnish

Broth
3 cups (l l) veal or chicken stock
1 oz (30 g) ginger root, grated
1 sprig coriander (cilantro)
6 coriander seeds
6 black peppercorns

Aromatic salt
4 teaspoons (20 g) sea salt
Zest of 1 lime, grated
4 coriander seeds
7 red peppercorns

1
Combine the ingredients for the broth in a saucepan, bring to the boil, then add the cabbage and poach it until cooked but slightly firm (crunchy). Drain it on a rack, reserving the poaching liquid Cut into four.

2
Season the foie gras with sea salt and peppercorns. Heat it in a sauté pan, then add the cabbage, onions, and slices of ginger. Continue cooking, regularly sprinkling with the cabbage poaching liquid.

3
Season the tuna with sea salt and peppercorns. Bake it on a griddle, just until firm so it retains its pink color.

4
When the foie gras is done (the temperature in the center should be 119°F/48°C), remove it and leave it to cool on a rack for 10 minutes. Remove 80 percent of the fat from the sauté pan, add the tuna, and deglaze with the lemon vinegar. Reduce the liquid for 1 minute, then moisten with a ladleful of the poaching liquid. Finish the ingredients with a little more meat juice, stirring to deglaze the contents of the pan. To serve, decorate with the coriander flowers and aromatic salt.

Recommended wine: Fitou 2001, Les Vendangeurs de la Violette, Jacques Guérin's Domaine les Mille Vignes.

BEEF
HEART
SPRING
CABBAGE,
poached with pan-
fried tuna and
foie gras

SWISS CHARD
by Joël

Swiss chard, like its close relative the beet, is the result of a series of mutations of *Beta maritima*, a lively little biennial with a very thin root and slightly fleshy leaves that still grows along the Atlantic and Mediterranean coasts of France. The hypertrophy of the flower stalk and thickening of the main rib of the leaf produces chard, or Swiss chard. In France, it is known as *bette à cardes*, and sometimes as *poirée*. The latter name is medieval, because chard was one of the two main ingredients in the thick vegetable stew known as *porée*, the other being leek. As with so many vegetables that are now cultivated by specialist growers, the finest leaves are the tender ones picked in the spring; they are planted in mid-March in our tunnels or cold frames and are ready for harvesting only five weeks later. The fragile young stems do not need to be peeled or trimmed, and they melt in the pan like butter in the sun. Once again, observation, understanding, and the correct interpretation of the way in which chard ages are essential in order to be able to harvest the plant when it is at its best and its optimum tenderness. The fibers should not be woody and should be as sweet and crunchy as in the beet. One of my favorite varieties is the green Ampuis variety, which has thick, crinkly leaves and thinner ribs and it is one of the spring varieties that is most prized by gourmets. CATHERINE GUERRAZ, chef and owner of CHEZ CATHERINE, understands this fragile and delicate plant only too well, and she is able to transform it into a divine dish. Here, she offers us a recipe from the Nice district, handed down to her by her mother-in-law, who comes from the area.

SWISS CHARD
by Catherine Guerraz

1

Soak the raisins or currants in warm water until they swell.

To make the filling, remove the ribs from the chard and discard them. You should now have about 5 cups (1 kg) of the chard. Blanch the leaves in boiling water for 2 minutes. Drain and press the leaves dry on kitchen paper, then shred them finely with a knife. After cooking, you should have around 2½ cups (300 g).

Put the cooked leaves in a bowl. Melt the butter and add while still hot, stirring it into the chard. Then add the grated Gruyère cheese and the petits-suisses or alternative. Crush the macaroon or amaretto cookie and add along with the pine nuts. Mix well, adding the olive oil, rum, orange-flower water, and a pinch of salt.

2

Olive oil dough

Sift the flour into a bowl, then beat in the rest of the ingredients for the dough and mix well. The dough should be smooth and supple and it ought not to weigh more than 1 lb 2 oz–1 lb 5 oz (500–600 g). Cover the dough with plastic wrap or a damp cloth and leave to rest in a cool place for at least 1 hour.

3

To make the pie, divide the dough into two equal pieces. Roll out the first piece with a rolling pin. Line the pie pan with nonstick baking paper or parchment paper. Cover this with the rolled-out dough, letting it overlap the edge of the pan so it can be firmly attached to the upper layer of dough.

4

Spread the chard filling over the dough in the pan, then cover with the soaked raisins, slices of apple, and greengage jam or preserve, and finish with a sprinkling of rum. Roll out the second piece of dough and use it to cover the filling. Seal it to the lower half of the dough, using the tines of a fork to crimp the edges.

5

Combine the ingredients for the glaze. Use a pastry brush to brush the glaze over the pastry; this will keep it supple during cooking. Prick the surface with the tines of a fork so the steam can escape during cooking.

Bake in a preheated 425°F (220°C) oven for 35 minutes. The pastry should turn golden-brown during cooking.

6

Remove the pie from the oven and sprinkle it with confectioner's sugar. Leave it to cool to room temperature before serving.

Recommended wine: Cassis Blanc, Clos Sainte-Magdeleine.

Serves 8

Filling
3 tablespoons (80 g) raisins or currants
6 lb 8 oz (3 kg) Swiss chard
⅓ cup (90 g) hot melted butter
3 tablespoons (50 g) freshly grated Gruyère cheese
2 petits-suisses, or ½ cup (125 ml) fromage frais or quark
1 macaroon or amaretto cookie
1 tablespoon pine nuts
2 tablespoons olive oil
2 tablespoons rum
2 tablespoons orange-flower water
1 pinch salt
2 russet apples, thinly sliced
1 pot greengage jam or preserve
1 tablespoon rum

Olive oil dough
2½ cups (300 g) all-purpose flour
4 tablespoons milk
1 tablespoon orange-flower water
4 tablespoons olive oil
2 tablespoons (30 g) melted butter
1 pinch salt
4 tablespoons water

Glaze
1 egg yolk
2 teaspoons (10 g) melted butter
1 tablespoon cream
4 tablespoons sifted confectioner's (powdered) sugar

1 x 14-in (35-cm) pie pan
Nonstick baking paper

SWISS CHARD **pie, Nice-style**

CHERRY BELLE

by Joël

RADISH

Cherry Belle radish

The radish is a traditional vegetable that can be traced way back in history; it featured on the menu of the builders of Khufu's pyramid in Egypt. It was also very popular in Delphi, Greece, where it was served on golden platters, while other root vegetables were served only on silver. It is found in mid-seventeenth century French books on horticulture under the name of *raifort*, a word now reserved for its less refined cousin, the horseradish. The baby radish is usually grown close to large towns since it does not travel well; the radish tops, so juicy when picked, soon fade and turn papery and yellow.

The round scarlet radish—ancestor of the cherry radish—and the oblong radish with a white tip have been the most frequently grown varieties in the Île-de-France from the nineteenth century onward. The cherry radish has flesh that is less dense and juicier than its elongated cousin. Contrary to popular belief, an entirely red skin does not necessarily mean that the radish is hot and peppery. The fieriness depends on the variety, the regularity with which the plant is watered and, finally—the one factor that cannot be controlled outdoors—the air temperature. When the weather is very hot, if you crunch on a little Cherry Belle radish, you will notice that the flesh is quite mild. However, when you finish chewing it, when all that remains are the fibers from the skin, you get a short, sharp shock, and you will need to extinguish the fire in your throat. That is why these little radishes are best eaten in the spring and in the fall in temperate climates.

To provide a recipe for this vegetable, I invited a chef who never fails to travel three or four times a week to visit my market stall to find exactly what he needs for his dishes. He is CHRISTOPHE PELÉ, chef of LE JARDIN, a restaurant at Royal Monceau. As usual, for this recipe, he came to my booth to choose the most perfect cherry radishes—picked that day—which, to use his favorite expression, had to be "tip-top"!

CHERRY BELLE
by Christophe Pelé
RADISH

Serves 4

4 live spider crabs
4 unflavored gelatin leaves
2 bunches Cherry Belle radishes with tops (to
obtain 2 cups/500 ml juice)
7 oz (200 g) wild garlic (ramson) leaves
Juice of 1 lime
2 tablespoons olive oil
Salt and pepper
3 tablespoons (40 g) flying-fish eggs
1 bunch chives, minced

1

Plunge the spider crabs into boiling water and boil for 4 minutes. Drain, then shell completely. Reserve the white flesh and the coral separately. Soak the gelatin leaves in cold water for 10 minutes.

2

Dice 12 radishes finely. Cut of all the tops of the remaining radishes and put the leaves in a bowl of ice water. Trim the radishes and put them through a juicer. Strain the juice (there should be 2 cups/500 ml) through a sieve. Warm the juice in a saucepan for a few seconds so that the gelatin will dissolve more easily. Remove from the heat (the juice must not be allowed to get too hot) and stir the gelatin leaves into it. Season with salt and pepper.

3

Blanch the radish tops with the wild garlic leaves in boiling water for 1 minute, then rinse in ice water. Drain, then grind in a food processor with the lime juice, olive oil, and some salt and pepper to obtain a pistou-like sauce.

4

Put a tablespoon of the pistou on a plate, season the spider crab claws and arrange them vertically in the center of the plate. Pour the radish jello round them (it should be fairly liquid and oily in appearance) and sprinkle it with the diced radishes. Arrange a small mound of flying-fish eggs and crab coral on the jello and sprinkle everything with the minced chives. Serve immediately.

Recommended wine: Saumur, Château Tour Grise 2002, Les Amandiers.

Spider crabs in CHERRY BELLE RADISH **jello, with a pistou of radish tops**

BUTTERHEAD LETTUCE
by Joël

Butterhead lettuce At our truck farm, lettuces grown in the open air are harvested from late April through late October. Every week, thousands of seedlings are pricked out and sown, reaching maturity thirty to sixty days later, depending on the season. At each planting, fourteen to twenty varieties are planted closely together, creating a checkerboard of irregular patches of color without any apparent order. The development and growth of each type of lettuce can be seen from week to week. The soil is carefully prepared, so that the lettuce roots expand rapidly. The leaf colors range from dark green to pale green, as well as reddish-brown, due to the anthocyan present in the plant. They gradually expand, as if staking their claim to the soil from which they get their nourishment. Among the voluminous Butter or Boston lettuces, the crunchy Batavia and Iceberg lettuces, the crinkly-leaved Lollo Rosso, and the frilly red Oakleaf lettuce, the Romaines stand straight and tall, as do the Belgian endives. There are two varieties of modest dimensions that seem determined to hold their ground and not give way to their invading neighbors. They are cousins, both originating from the south of France. The russet one is known as Rougette du Midi; it has a rounded head with soft foliage and a strong flavor. The other, the Sucrine, is both rounded and tall, since its dense ball of leaves tends to grow upward. I love it for the texture of its thick yet tender leaves, its tight, crunchy heart, and its mild flavor. As the perfect vegetable for a warm summer evening, how could we not succumb to the delightful freshness that is conveyed through its leaves?

This lettuce being a native of the south, I could only give it to a chef who is from the Midi, although she is now exercising her talents in Paris. She is HÉLÈNE DARROZE, chef and owner of her restaurant. We are greatly indebted to her for contributing her art and renown to the conquest—or rather, the re-conquest—of a certain parity between the sexes in the world of haute cuisine.

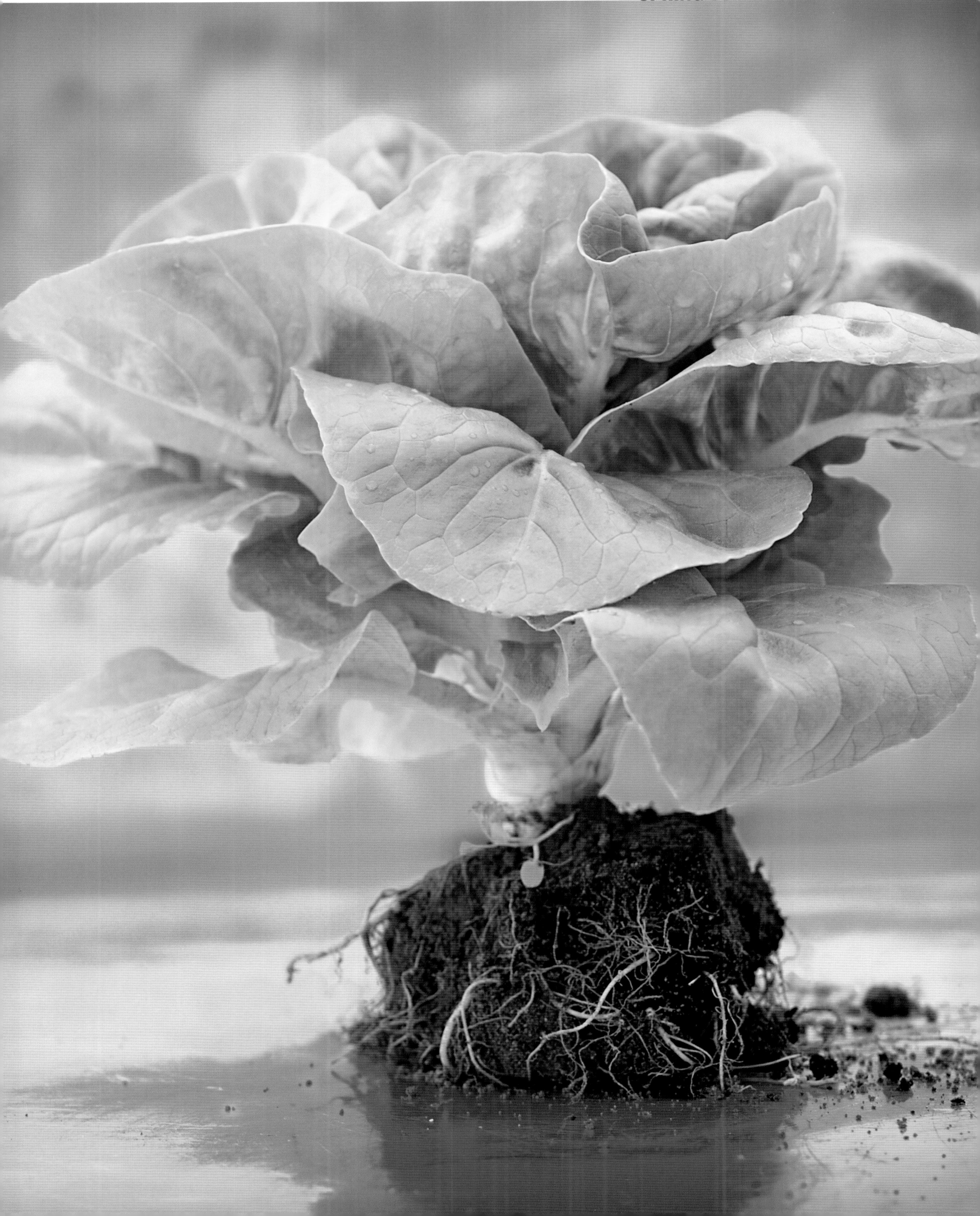

BUTTERHEAD
by Hélène Darroze
LETTUCE

1
Whipped sheep's-milk yogurt cream
Combine and blend all the ingredients for the cream. Strain them and pour them into a whipped cream dispenser or piping bag. Chill until required.

2
Cut the lettuce into quarters. Season with the sea salt and chili powder and sprinkle with olive oil.

3
Arrange the lettuce on plates. Pipe the whipped cream onto each lettuce quarter, and place a boquerone anchovy on top.

Recommended wine: Madiran 1999, Pierre Speyer.

Serves 4

4 butterhead lettuces
¼ teaspoon (3 g) sea salt
¼ teaspoon (2 g) ground birdseye chili pepper
4 tablespoons (50 ml) olive oil
4 boquerone anchovies

Whipped sheep's milk yogurt cream
⅓ cup (100 ml) sheep's milk yogurt
4 tablespoons (50 ml) whipping cream
Dash of chili powder

BUTTERHEAD LETTUCE **with boquerone anchovies**

PURPLE BABY ARTICHOKE

by Joël

Artichoke cultivation in France only began two centuries ago. The artichoke is the descendant of two types of wild thistle or cardoon. It came to France from the western Mediterranean, somewhere between Africa and modern-day Spain. Although there is anecdotal evidence that the Italian queen of France Catherine de' Medici was particularly fond of artichokes, and that they were eaten during the Renaissance, it was not until 1850 that production was developed commercially. Since then, the artichoke has seen periods of great popularity followed by serious decline, the consequence of which has been the concentration of its cultivation in regions with the most favorable climate. In the Île-de-France—the agricultural region that has so long been responsible for feeding the French capital—the variety traditionally grown has been the Vert de Laon, which is reproduced by replanting cuttings of leaf buds emerging from old stumps. On my truck farm, I continue to grow some hundreds of plants of this very old variety, since it has excellent gustatory qualities, but it tends to mature late and its low yield makes it an expensive vegetable to grow. The newly developed varieties, bred from the pale green Hyères varieties and the Violet of Provence, can be grown from seed. This greater diversity of cultivars makes it easier to expand our production calendar and thus the range of possible uses for the vegetable. Concerto, one of the baby violet types that were once only grown in the French Midi, produces tender leaves that we pick the day before taking them to market. To ensure the finest quality, we need to water them heavily, especially just before harvest, and we also have to pick the heads when the color of the leaves is at its most intense.

OLIVIER GUYON, head chef of the restaurant GOUMARD in Paris, seeks out these artichokes at our booth each market day. As he chooses the vegetables he needs for his current menu, he enthusiastically explains to me how he cooks them, thus giving me a host of useful information that will help me to fine-tune my production techniques. I am—and always have been—a food-lover and I feel no shame in admitting that just reading the following recipe makes my mouth water.

PURPLE BABY ARTICHOKE

by Olivier Guyon

1
White truffle sorbet

Make a syrup by boiling the water and sugar. Leave it to cool until cold, then combine with the sheep's milk yogurt, white truffle, and truffle oil. Make the sorbet in a Pacojet twice, so that it is very smooth, or stir it for 25 to 30 minutes in another standard ice cream-maker, and freeze until required.

2
Milk jelly

Peel the artichokes, reserving the leaves and discarding the chokes. Pour the milk into a saucepan, add the artichoke leaves, anise, and pink garlic. Bring to the boil, leave to infuse for 10 minutes, then strain through a conical sieve. Incorporate the gelatin and pour out onto a jellyroll pan. Spread evenly and leave to set.

3
Artichoke pulp

Heat the olive oil and lightly sauté the artichokes. Add 1 scant cup (200 ml) water, cover the pan, and steam on low heat. When they are done, grind them in a food processor with a tablespoon of olive oil and the cooking juice until you have a smooth pulp. Spread it out on a work surface and use a cookie cutter to cut rounds from it.

4
Socca (chickpea cookie)

To make the socca, mix the chickpea flour, olive oil, warm water, salt, and pepper. When the batter is smooth and liquid, pour it into a nonstick omelet pan and cook on fairly low heat as you would a crêpe. Brown for

2–3 minutes on each side. Use a cookie cutter to cut out rounds about ¾ inches (7 cm) in diameter.

5

Shell the crawfish body. Crack the claws, reserving the meat, and roll up the claw meat using a wooden cocktail stick. Reserve it.

6

Slice thinly the raw artichokes. Use a cookie-cutter to cut a thin round from the jello. Sauté the crawfish.

7
Assembling the dish

Place overlapping circles of artichoke pulp on a dish to create a rosette shape. Place a socca on top and then another layer of artichoke pulp and socca. Place a slice of jello on top. Arrange the slices of artichoke on top, finishing with a crawfish. Place a scoop of the white truffle sorbet on the side and serve immediately.

Recommended wine: Saumur Blanc, Cuvée Les Clos 2002, Domaine Guiberteau.

Serves

4 large crawfish cooke
with their claw
12 purple baby artichoke

White truffle sorbe
1 cup (250 g) suga
1 cup (250 ml) wate
2½ cups (5 pots) sheep's milk yogu
2 teaspoons (10 g) grated whi
truffl
⅔ cup (150 ml) white truffle o

Milk jell
2 handfuls artichoke leaves (about
medium artichoke
1 scant cup (200 ml) mi
1 handful (about ¼ cup) anis
1 Lautrec pink garlic clo
3 leaves unflavored gelat

Artichoke pul
12 purple baby artichok
3½ tablespoons (50 ml) olive o

Socca (chickpea cookie
⅔ cup (100 g) chickpea flou
½ cup (100 ml) olive o
1 scant cup (200 ml) warm wat
Salt and black peppe

PURPLE BABY ARTICHOKE **pulp with baked crawfish, milk jelly infused with artichoke leaves and anise, crunchy chickpea cookie, and white truffle sorbet**

SUMMER SPROUTING BROCCOLI

by Joël

Summer sprouting broccoli The vegetable known as "broccoli" has long been confused with the cauliflower, but should be used correctly to refer to all the "branched" flowering cabbages. In fact, what is commonly sold as broccoli should technically be known as "calabrese," a type that has a fairly compact head, distinguishing it from the bunched broccoli more often grown in the Vendée, the area in the center of the Atlantic coast of France. The quality of the flower head varies because it can develop very quickly, depending on the weather. The plant needs regular watering, especially during hot spells. The separation of the head from the rest of the plant during harvesting does not necessarily arrest the flowering, and sometimes, even if the heads are left overnight in the cold store, I come along in the morning to find yellowed heads that have fully blossomed. The Arcadia variety belongs to the blue-green type. It is preferred to the pale green which, for some reason, is supposed to be less fresh, though this is usually not the case. It is important to know that a freshly picked stem supporting the head can be cooked separately, in order to extract what some people call the "cabbage marrow," as if it were bone marrow.

MICHEL TROISGROS the world-famous chef, manages his famous MAISON TROISGROS in Roanne, a temple of French gastronomy, but recently opened LA TABLE DU LANCASTER in Paris. He has agreed to reveal some of his secrets of cooking with broccoli. Let us see how one of the most brilliant chefs of his generation can still surprise us using calabrese.

SUMMER SPROUTING
by Michel Troisgros
BROCCOLI

1

Make a tomato sauce or use a high quality canned product. Incorporate the calamari ink into it.
Bring a large pan of salted water to the boil and cook the broccoli until it is "al dente." Cut the heads in half.

2

Cut the crusts off the bread and slice it thinly, then use a cookie cutter to cut it into rounds.

3

Clean the calamari pouch and score diamond shapes into it, then cut them out. Refrigerate until required.

4

Heat all but 2 tablespoons of the peanut oil and deep-fry the sage leaves. Drain on absorbent paper and sprinkle with salt. Beat the egg with a fork, adding a pinch of salt.

5

Dip each halved broccoli head into the beaten egg and stick one bread round onto each one. Heat the rest of the peanut oil in a nonstick frying pan and add the broccoli and bread, bread-side down. Fry until golden, then turn over and cook for a few more moments. Sprinkle with pepper.

6

Season the calamari pieces and heat the olive oil. Sauté the calamari on high heat until cooked through.

7

Arrange three broccoli halves side by side on a serving platter. Put three dabs of the ink-and-tomato sauce on one side. Arrange the calamari on the sauce and the sage leaves on the other side.

Recommended wine: Jasnières 2002, Domaine de Bellivière, owned by Éric Nicolas.

Serves

1 cup (250 ml) good tomato sauc
A few drops calamari in
2 heads summer sprouting brocco
¼ of a day-old sandwich lo
1 calamari poud
1 scant cup (200 ml) peanut o
12 fresh sage leave
1 eg
Olive o
Salt and peppe

SUMMER SPROUTING BROCCOLI **with calamari and its ink**

CORIANDER FLOWER

by Joël

Coriander flower Coriander is one of those plants that could be granted the title of "universal aromatic" due to its presence in all regions of the globe. Coriander may also be the most ancient herb still in common use: traces of it have been found in the tombs of Egyptian pharaohs. Coriander (cilantro) has become a universal herb in cookery, although one of its names in English is dizzicorn, due to its narcotic effects on the body if eaten in huge quantities. In fact, over the centuries, all sorts of medicinal and even aphrodisiac properties have been ascribed to coriander, though it has also been said to be diabolical and harmful.

We grow coriander at our truck farm purely for cookery purposes. It is a very versatile plant, and all parts of it are edible. The seeds are often ground or powdered and used to flavor a number of dishes. They have a mild taste, slightly reminiscent of citrus. The young leaves that look so much like those of flat-leafed parsley are used in salads and sauces. The more mature the herb, the stronger the flavor. When coriander begins to resemble dillweed, another umbelliferous plant, the roots can be harvested and used as they are, or crushed and combined with garlic, as it often is in Asia. The plant produces abundant white flowers which can also be used in cookery. ANTOINE MEYSSONNIER and RAIMUNDO BRIONES run the company HAUT DU PANIER, which delivers my vegetables to individual customers every Friday. I asked them to display their talents as cooks and their ideas for using the lovely white flowers of this herb.

CORIANDER

by Antoine Meyssonnier & Raimundo Briones

FLOWER

1

Beet syrup

Peel and dice the 2 beets. Bring the water and vinegar to the boil, and simmer the beets for 10 minutes, then add the sugar, coriander seeds, lime zest, and the ¼ bunch of coriander flowers.
Push through a sieve and incorporate the lime juice Reduce the liquid until it has a syrupy consistency.

2

Preheat the oven to 400°F (200°C). Line two cookie sheets with nonstick baking paper. Use a mandolin slicer to slice the third beet into very thin slices. Brush the beet slices with olive oil on both sides, placing them on the nonstick baking paper when done. Bake for 10 minutes. Remove them from the oven and sprinkle with a few Szechuan peppercorns and sea salt.

3

Slice the sea bass fillet into thin strips, retaining only the white flesh. Crumble the cauliflower tops. Put them in a Dutch oven with the sea bass and add a little olive oil, the sweet almond oil, sea salt, Szechuan peppercorns, and the ⅓ bunch of coriander flowers.

4

Assembling the dish

Arrange three towers on a plate as follows: on each slice of beet, place the equivalent of a large teaspoon of a mixture of cauliflower, bass, and coriander flowers. Cover with another round of beet and sprinkle coriander flowers over it and around the plate.
Finally, pour a trail of beet syrup around the towers.

Recommended wine: White Côte-de-Beaune burgundy, Grande Châtelaine 2002, from Emmanuel Giboulot.

Serves 4

Beet syrup
2 raw red beets
1 scant cup (200 ml) mineral water or seltzer
2½ cups (600 ml) Banyuls wine vinegar
4 teaspoons (20 g) sugar
Coriander seeds
Zest of 1 lime, grated
¼ bunch of coriander flowers
Juice of ½ lime, squeezed

1 raw red beet
Szechuan pepper
Sea salt
2¼ lb (1 x 1 kg) line-caught sea bass
¼ small cauliflower
3 tablespoons olive oil
1 tablespoon sweet almond oil
⅓ bunch coriander flowers

CORIANDER FLOWERS, sea bass, and beet cookies

DWARF
GREEN BEAN

by Joël

The first green beans

The first green beans were brought back by the navigators who discovered the Americas, and more specifically Central America. Fresh green beans, the French beans we know today, were the result of careful selection by European growers and horticulturalists who were already familiar with the cultivation of fresh broad beans and garden peas. In fact, until the coming of railroad transport in the mid-nineteenth century, green beans were produced in the Paris region even in the depths of winter by using various clever devices such as heated layers under cold frames and lots of inexpensive labor. Nowadays, we sow the first seeds in March under our high polytunnels, and generally start harvesting around May 20. Morgane, one of my favorite varieties, is created and distributed by the Clause company. It belongs to the string bean type that produces a long cylindrical pod. It only becomes stringy if the bean is harvested too late, or if the wrong kind of weather cannot be compensated for by the skill of the growers; for instance, by watering in the early morning during a hot, dry spell. Manual picking is slow and arduous, despite the fact that the variety has a high yield. This is the reason why these beans are so expensive in comparison with those that can be harvested mechanically. The best of these green beans are picked by hand on the day before they are taken to market. The pod is friable but tender, the flesh is melting with a strong but delicate flavor. All these qualities cannot be achieved in the baby green beans that are machine-harvested, even though there have been improvements in recent years. On the other hand, manual picking in our part of the world is in danger of disappearing, in view of the high cost and the ever-decreasing number of people who are skilled enough to do it. Once again, it will be the best of our locally grown produce that will disappear. MANUEL MARTINEZ, chef and owner of the RELAIS LOUIS XIII in Paris, who practices his art in such a historical setting, struck me as being the perfect person to cook this vegetable, picked so young but steeped in the evolutions of our society.

DWARF

by Manuel Martinez

GREEN BEAN

Serves 4

1¾ cups (400 g) dwarf green beans
3 tablespoons aged sherry vinegar
1 tablespoon almond oil
Salt and pepper
1 tablespoon chopped chervil

1 lobster (around 1 lb 2 oz/500 g), shelled
4 eggs
1 tablespoon wine vinegar
4 anchovy fillets
4 slices tuna in oil

1
Cook the green beans in plenty of boiling water. Refresh them by plunging them into ice water, then drain them. Reserve until required.

2
Make the dressing by combining the sherry vinegar, almond oil, salt, pepper, and chopped chervil. Toss the beans in the dressing.

3
Slice the lobster and steam it for 10 minutes.
To soft-boil the eggs, bring a pot of water to the boil and add the wine vinegar. Add the eggs and cook for 4 minutes. Stop the cooking by pouring cold water over them. Shell them under a thin stream of cold water and reserve them.

4
Assembling the dish
Place a cluster of green beans in the center of the dish. Arrange the anchovies and tuna on top. Arrange the lobster and soft-boiled egg around the center. Serve well chilled.

Recommended wine: Domaine des Aspes, Viognier La Mouline 2002.

DWARF GREEN BEANS **and Breton lobster with almond oil dressing**

WARTY RIDGE CUCUMBER

by Joël

Warty Ridge cucumber A common garden plant, the Warty Ridge cucumber has rough-textured, dark green skin. Yet from the first mouthfuls of its cool, pleasant flavor and crunchy flesh, it is highly pleasurable. This vegetable sausage can be eaten raw or pickled in brine or vinegar. When sown in the open air, two successive plantings are needed to ensure continuous production from June through October. This means that if there are long periods of wet weather, there is a risk of oidium—the fungal disease that causes rot—or if the weather is too hot and dry for long spells, the fruits can be hollow and sometimes bitter. The natural bitterness of the cucumber is due to the presence of curcubitacins throughout the plant that become more pronounced depending on the conditions of growth and the environment. I prefer to grow this relative of the squash in a glasshouse with its root in the earth, attaching the plant by a string to the metal frame of the glasshouse. When suspended in this way, cucumbers grow straighter, making them easier to use in the kitchen. The flesh is more uniform and there is no bitterness because each plant receives just the right amount of water daily through a watering system. The difference between the Warty Ridge cucumber and those cucumbers that are grown hydroponically is unquestionably in the strength of flavor.

To bring out the best in this vegetable that has been cultivated since Ancient Egyptian times and cooked in almost every way possible, I sought a recipe created and executed by ANTOINE WESTERMANN, chef and owner of the restaurant BUEREHIESEL in Strasbourg and his partner and disciple ANTONY CLÉMOT, chef of the Parisian restaurant MON VIEIL AMI. These two piano virtuosos combined their four expert hands to reveal a new way of cooking with cucumbers.

WARTY RIDGE
by Antoine Westermann & Antony Clémot
CUCUMBER

1
Crabs (preferably Dungeness or Devon)
Add the pot herbs to a large pot of boiling water and add the crabs. Cook for around 10 minutes, then remove from the pot and leave to cool. Shell the crabs. Sauté the chopped shallots and garlic in butter. Add the pieces of crab, then the chopped chives.
To make the sour sauce, combine the orange and lemon juice with the other ingredients. Mix this sauce with the crabmeat. Check the seasoning and reserve.

2
Cucumber cannelloni
Slice the cucumbers lengthwise into very thin strips using a mandolin slicer (the slices should be 1/8-inch/ 2-mm thick maximum). Sprinkle the slices with salt and leave them for about 1 hour to release their liquid. Rinse them under cold running water.
Arrange 4 slices of cucumber per portion side by side on a piece of plastic wrap. Divide the crabmeat mixture into four portions and place on the cucumber pieces, then roll up the plastic wrap into a cylinder. Refrigerate until required.

3
Topping
Mix all the topping ingredients together and pour the liquid over the cucumber cannelloni.

Recommended wine: Riesling Osterberg 2001, from André Kientzler at Ribeauvillé.

Serve

2 crabs weighing ab
2¼ lb (1 kg) ea
3 shallots, chopp
1 garlic clo
¼ cup (50 g) but
1 bunch chives, chopp

Pot herb
(for the crab bo
1 car
1 oni
1 le
Thy
Bay le

Sour sauc
Juice of 1 oran
Juice of 1 lem
2 tablespoons (30 ml) sherry vineg
2 tablespoons (30 ml) soy sau
4 tablespoons (60 ml) olive
1 pinch papri
1 pinch ging

3 Warty Ridge cucumb

Toppi
4 teaspoons (20 ml) hor
1 teaspoon (4 ml) soy
Juice of 1 lem

WARTY RIDGE CUCUMBER **and crab cannelloni in sour sauce**

LONG RED BEET
by Joël

Beet, or beetroot, is a tap root that may be round or carrot-shaped. Although usually ruby red, it can also be white, yellow, or even candy-striped. In the Île-de-France, beets can't be sown before the first spring days. Even if you just intend to eat baby beets in a salad, you'll have to wait until early summer before lifting the roots. They will still be immature, but already tender and sweet. Among the multicolored plants, you will easily recognize the variety that is in the least hurry to ripen. The variety Cylindra is a demi-long variety, a little like the French variety known as Crapaudine. Crapaudine, meaning toad-like one, is wrinkled from early youth. It has an irregular, spindle-shaped root, with a dark skin that is similar to its ancestor, the variety known as Castelnaudary, whose delicate flesh and hazelnut flavor it has retained. It is lifted in mid-October, then stripped of its leaves. I keep it as it is, still covered in dirt, in a cold store. It stays there in a temperature of 35.6°F (2 °C), the ambient air being saturated with water so as to prevent it from wilting. After a period of dormancy, it proves itself to be in "good health" by showing a few young shoots around the neck. It is now time to hand it over to my friend PIERRE HERMÉ so he can demonstrate the intimate relationship this delicious vegetable has with the territory on which it has developed. This brilliant patissier marries it with other fruits of the earth in order to produce a dessert whose secret he now shares with us.

LONG RED BEET
by Pierre Hermé

Serves 8

Strawberry marshmallow
4 tablespoons (50 g) cornstarch
4 tablespoons (50 g) confectioner's sugar
4 tablespoons (20 g) unflavored gelatin (2 leaves)
2 teaspoons (10 g) glucose; 1 cup (250 g) sugar; ½ cup (120 ml) water
3 oz (80 g) egg whites
6 tablespoons (75 g) concentrated strawberry purée (Garnier)
2 tablespoons (30 ml) lemon juice; a few drops pink coloring

Beets cooked in strawberry juice
1 cup (200 g) cooked beets; 3 tablespoons (50 g) sugar;
⅓ cup (100 ml) water, 1 cup (250 g) strawberry purée

Strawberry compote
1½ teaspoons (8 g) unflavored gelatin (4 leaves)
1¾ cups (400 g) strawberry purée; 2¼ oz (60 g) superfine sugar

Poppy syrup custard
1 teaspoon (4 g) unflavored gelatin (2 leaves); 3 egg yolks,
2 tablespoons (35 ml) poppy syrup; 1 cup (220 ml) light cream

Mascarpone cream with poppy syrup
1 cup (250 ml) poppy syrup custard (*see step 4*)
1¾ cups (330 g) mascarpone; 5 tablespoons (80 ml) poppy syrup

Strawberries and beets in strawberry juice
1 cup (200 g) beets cooked in strawberry juice (*see step 2*)
1½ cups (300 g) fresh strawberries, diced

1
Strawberry marshmallow (prepare two days before)

Sift the cornstarch and confectioner's sugar. Soak the gelatin in cold water. Cook the glucose with the sugar and water to 243°F (117°C), then leave to cool to 226°F (108°C). Whip the egg whites into stiff peaks and fold the cooled syrup into them, beating constantly. Leave this meringue to cool. Drain the gelatin and melt it with a little of the strawberry purée. Add the rest of the strawberry purée, the pink coloring, and the lemon juice and pour the mixture in a stream into the cooled meringue.

On a silicone baking sheet placed on a jellyroll pan, spread out the mixture to a thickness of ½ inch (1 cm). Sprinkle the surface with half the cornstarch and confectioner's sugar mixture. Dry overnight at a temperature of 77°F (25°C) in a room with low humidity. The next day, unmold the marshmallow and repeat the drying operation.

After 48 hours of drying, slice the strawberry marshmallow into ½-inch (1-cm) cubes. Sprinkle these cubes with the other half of the cornstarch and confectioner's sugar mixture. Place them in a sieve to shake off the excess. Store them in a cool place, away from humidity.

2
Beets cooked in strawberry juice (prepare the day before)

Peel the beets and cook them in a pressure cooker. Leave to cool, and as soon as they are cool, dice them into ½ inch (1 cm) cubes and place them in a colander. Boil the sugar and water and add the strawberry purée and beet cubes. Bring to the boil, skim the surface to remove any film, and leave to cool before storing. It is important to let the beets macerate in the strawberry syrup for at least 24 hours before use.

3
Strawberry compote

Soak the gelatin in cold water. Melt the gelatin and mix in a little strawberry purée. Then add the rest of the purée and the sugar, beating hard with a whisk. Leave to cool at room temperature. Pour into cocktail glasses just before the jello can set.

4
Poppy syrup custard

Soak the gelatin in cold water for at least 20 minutes. Beat the egg yolks with the poppy syrup. Bring the cream to the boil and add it to the yolks and syrup, then simmer, as for a custard. Add the drained gelatin, mix well, and leave to cool.

5

Mascarpone cream with poppy syrup

Lightly beat the custard to make it smooth. Loosen the mascarpone with the poppy syrup, then incorporate the custard into the mixture, folding it in with a rubber spatula. Use immediately.

6

Strawberries and beets in strawberry juice

Drain the beets cooked in strawberry juice from step 2. Add the cubed strawberries to the drained beets.

7

Assembling the dish

Take the cocktail glasses with the strawberry compote. Add the strawberries and beets cooked in strawberry juice, then cover with the mascarpone cream with poppy syrup. Arrange the strawberry marshmallow cubes on the poppy syrup cream. Refrigerate for 1 hour until ready to eat and eat within 24 hours

Recommended drinks: water, coffee, tea, Dry Rosé de Saignée Champagne, Duval-Leroy.

Playful Spirit (compote of strawberries, mascarpone cream with poppy syrup, strawberries and LONG RED BEETS **in strawberry juice, with strawberry marshmallow)**

TAXI

by Joël

ZUCCHINI

Taxi zucchini I chose Taxi, a recently developed American variety of zucchini, as a reminder that this vegetable was one of those brought to Europe by Christopher Columbus from the New World. In Europe, this squash quickly supplanted the gourds and calabashes that still grow wild in Africa. The zucchini is an immature fruit of the Cucurbitaceae family, a member of the genus *Cucurbita,* and more specifically the *pepo* species and finally the zucchini group. There are hundreds of varieties grown all over the globe. Although usually elongated, there are some that are round, such as the Eight Ball; others that are dark green or yellow, like the Fructidor, and yet others that are pale green, as in the French Ronde de Nice variety, though the latter are really members of the squash family. It is a pity that the potential resulting from the diversity of shapes, colors, and even textures and flavors is not more frequently manifested on our plates. The art of cooking is not helped by the trend toward standardization, whereby a vegetable is judged on external factors such as size and regularity of shape. The systematic elimination of fruits and vegetables that show even the tiniest signs of weather damage has also contributed to the consumer being less than familiar with unusual produce. He or she is often forced to choose on the basis of labels or brands that merely define technical specifications. Local growers selling their produce directly to the consumer are the last bastion of good taste, able to reveal and explain the benefits of a large range of produce which those cooks who are passionate about vegetables are only too happy to transform into delicious fare.

The micro-zucchini, still attached to the female flower, is the latest "vegetable sensation" among many Parisian chefs. A lot of recipes have been created for it, and WILLIAM LEDEUIL, chef and owner of the restaurant ZE KITCHEN GALERIE showed us how flowers and fruit from the same vegetable can be combined in a dish. It was instructive to note how my daughter Pauline—a food-lover if ever there was one— gobbled up the dish as soon as the photography had been completed. Excited and delighted with what she had glimpsed in the kitchen of the "Kitchen," she suggested trying some more of William's recipes the moment she came home.

TAXI
ZUCCHINI

by William Ledeuil

Serves 4

Zucchini soup
5 Taxi zucchini
2 Cévennes sweet onions
3 garlic cloves
2 fresh turmeric roots
3 sprigs lemongrass
1 birdseye chili pepper
4 teaspoons (20 ml) olive oil
1 scant cup (200 ml) chicken broth
⅓ cup (100 ml) coconut milk
Seasoning

Burrata
⅔ cup (150 g) burrata cheese
2 tablespoons olive oil
6 new purple onions (scallions)
Sea salt
Freshly ground black pepper

Arugula emulsion
3½ oz (100 g) wild arugula
¼ cup (50 ml) vegetable broth
¼ cup (50 ml) milk
4 teaspoons (20 ml) olive oil
Celery salt
1 soft-boiled egg

Garnish
4 two-colored zucchini
4 green zucchini
5 Taxi zucchini skins
6 tablespoons (80 ml) tempura batter
4 zucchini blossoms
Salt and pepper

1
Zucchini soup
Peel and slice the yellow zucchini, reserving the skins. Chop the onion, garlic, turmeric, lemongrass, and chili pepper, then heat the olive oil in a saucepan and cook on a low heat. Add oil to a frying pan and quickly sauté the zucchini, then drain them. Add them to the vegetable mix and season to taste. Cover the saucepan and cook on low heat for 30 minutes in order to obtain a soft mixture, like a preserve. Add the chicken broth and coconut milk and cook for a further 15 minutes. Grind in the food processor, season to taste, strain the mixture, and keep it in a cool place for 3 hours.

2
Burrata
Slice the burrata cheese and marinate it in the olive oil. Slice the onion bulbs and leaves and add them. Season with salt and pepper.

3
Arugula emulsion
Combine the arugula with the vegetable broth, milk, olive oil, a pinch of celery salt, and the soft-boiled egg. Strain and reserve.

4
Assembling and finishing the dish
Slice the zucchini and the reserved yellow zucchini skins into thin strips. Dip them in the tempura batter and fry them. Pour the zucchini soup into shallow soup bowls, arrange the burrata on top, and pour the arugula emulsion over it. Serve with the fried zucchini and the blossoms.

Recommended wine: Coteaux-du-Languedoc, Domaine Clavel Cascaille.

TAXI ZUCCHINI **soup with burrata and zucchini tempura**

GREEN ZEBRA
by Joël
TOMATO

Green Zebra tomato *Lycopersicon esculentum!* Yes, that's the one! You may well know it under its common name of tomato, but between its common name and the botanical name that translates as "edible wolf's peach," it goes by many other names. Among these are *"pomodoro"* (golden apple), a reference to the first tomatoes to reach Europe which were yellow, or "love apple," for the claims that it had aphrodisiac effects. For two centuries, like most of the Solanacea family that arrived from the New World or the distant lands of Asia, the tomato was shunned, suspected of being a product of the devil. It is certainly true that it must have been difficult to understand how the fruit of a plant that was known to be toxic, even deadly, could be perfectly edible. But after a slow start, things got moving quickly. The tomato conquered Europe and even North America, Asia, and the rest of the world. Today, it is one of the most popular vegetables in the world. The tomato is considered a vegetable from an economic point of view, but botanically speaking it is actually a fruit. It has a special place on my truck farm—and in my heart! It is the queen of summer, and continues to rule sometimes even as late as December. Quite a few gourmets come from afar to shop at my market stall: they like the fact that we grow this "magical" fruit quite traditionally, with its feet in the earth. It is planted in our polytunnels so that it cannot be damaged by hailstorms or other bad weather conditions. There are also other advantages to growing tomatoes under cover, but not forcing them. The plants are carefully irrigated by drip-feeding, to prevent the fruits becoming waterlogged and thus losing their flavor and fragrance.

The other reason I am particularly fond of this fruit-vegetable is more personal. Without it, I would certainly not be in the process of writing this book with Patrick and Lyndsay Mikanowski, because it was on the occasion of the publication of their first book, *Tomate*, that we met, and a friendship was born that still links us today.

The Green Zebra variety is a tomato that comes straight from my collection. For this recipe I have chosen someone who is enthusiastic about this fruit, someone who is also the kind of friend everyone would love to have. TAÏRA KURIHARA is the chef and owner of TAÏRA, a seafood restaurant (as can be seen from his sign) in Paris. This retiring individual—his brightly colored chef's shirts and pants are his only extravagance!—friendly and patient, is a true creator, with a sensitivity that enables him to stray from the well-trodden path. In terms of working with our vegetables, he is one of the most experienced—though not the oldest—chefs, and everyone on our sales team adores him for his kindness.

GREEN ZEBRA TOMATO
by Taïra Kurihara

Layers of crawfish, scallops, and green tomato jello

1

Grind the crawfish heads and claws in a food processor. Infuse the mixture in the rice milk over a low heat with a little salt, and strain through a conical sieve. Add the kuzu (or potato starch), stirring it into the infusion while it is still warm. Refrigerate until required.

2

Season a pan of water with sea salt and a few drops of red wine vinegar or lemon juice. Poach the 8 whole crawfish and 4 scallops just below the boil until cooked through.

3

Shell the crawfish and scallops and marinate them in a mixture of white balsamic vinegar, soy sauce, Vietnamese fish sauce (nuoc-mâm), salt, and sugar.

4

Soak the gelatin in cold water. Blanch and skin the tomatoes, halve them crosswise, and scoop out the juice and seeds. Reserve the tomato shells and heat the juice and seeds on low heat. Add the softened gelatin, stirring until dissolved. Strain and refrigerate until required.

5
Assembling the dish

Pour the crawfish and rice milk broth into 4 sundae glasses. Arrange layers of half the Green Zebra halves, poached crayfish, and sliced scallops. Top each sundae glass with half a tomato and place a spoonful of salmon roe inside. Carefully pour the Green Zebra jello around it.

Asparagus and shizo crunch

1

Wash the asparagus and use a mandolin slicer to slice the stem lengthwise into 4 strips. Refrigerate until required.

2

Chop the 2 shizo leaves finely.

3

Unroll the phyllo dough sheet and cut it into 4 rectangles measuring 3 x 8 inches (7 x 20 cm).

4

Brush each rectangle with a pastry brush dipped in water. Then place on it 1 strip of asparagus and half a chopped shizo leaf. Roll up the dough into a long cylindrical shape.

5

Heat the oil to 275°F (140°C). Plunge the phyllo dough cylinders into the oil and deep-fry them until they color. Drain on absorbent paper. Place a crunchy deep-fried pastry on the side of each sundae glass.

Recommended wine: Chinon Blanc 2004, Couly Dutheil.

Serves

Layers of crayfish and scallop
with Green Zebra jell
1¼ lb (500 g) crawfish heads and claw
2 cups (500 ml) rice milk (¼ cup/50 g rice cooked in 2 cups/500 ml mil
4 teaspoons (20 g) kuzu or potato star
Sea salt and red wine vineg
8 crawfish large enough to get 8–10 to the pound (16–20 to the k
4 scallo
2 tablespoons white balsamic vineg
1 teaspoon soy sau
A few drops Vietnamese fish sauce (nuoc-mâr
1 teaspoon sug
1 gelatin le
4 Green Zebra tomato
2 oz (50 g) salmon r

Asparagus and shizo crunc
1 green asparag
2 shizo leav
1 sheet phyllo dou
Peanut oil for deep-fryi

GREEN ZEBRA TOMATOES, layers of crawfish and scallops, with a Green Zebra
jello and asparagus and shizo crunch

SLIM JIM
EGGPLANT

by Joël

Slim Jim eggplant The eggplant was called "mad apple" when it first arrived in France, due to confusion with its poisonous cousins such as deadly nightshade and mandrake. It came from northern India, at least in its cultivated forms. In its native land, it features in many local dishes and is known as the queen of vegetables. It is mainly sold in its familiar deep violet color, whether rounded or elongated; however, looking through seed catalogs from abroad, or wandering through markets in other countries, it is not unusual to find white, pink, or green eggplants. Its shape can also vary: it can be oval, long, very thin, or even twisted into a corkscrew shape, like the Ping-tung, a Chinese variety from Taiwan. The Japanese varieties, which should be picked when very young and small, are dark in color, with an anthocyanic calyx surrounded by a paler fringe. They are no less surprising than the varieties that resemble white eggs, the reason that the first of these vegetables to reach England were dubbed "eggplants." I have been growing eggplant since the late 1970s and have learned to know and appreciate it in all its forms and colors, as well as enjoying the melting texture of the Asian varieties, the density of the white varieties, and the fleshiness of the violet-colored eggplants grown in Provence. Not forgetting the woodland mushroom flavors of the smoky Japanese varieties, the sweet, even sugary, varieties of round Italian eggplants or the faintly bitter flavor of green Indian eggplant. In the Paris region, I grow eggplant in polytunnels to shelter it from the vagaries of the weather. This ensures early harvests in June, which may last right up until early November, but it is quite feasible for you to grow them in your own garden in many regions. Be careful though, this "princess" is aggressive, and sharp spines on the calyx and the leaves lie in wait for the unwary picker. In fact, one of the indicators of freshness when selecting eggplant from a market cart is the sharpness of its spines—five or six days after picking, they droop and become floppy and inoffensive. ÉRIC BRIFFARD, chef and manager of the ÉLYSÉES restaurant at the Vernet Hotel in Paris, will deal with this beauty, which needs to be handled by an intelligent and creative chef.

SLIM JIM
by Éric Briffard
EGGPLANT

Serve

4 medium Slim Jim eggpl
(about 4–5 oz/120–150
3 garlic clo
6 tablespoons (90 ml) olive
1 pinch curry pow
1 sprig thy
Juice of ½ lem
2 white mini-eggpl
4 purple mini-eggpl
2 tablespoons (30 g) all-purpose fl
Salt, sea salt, freshly ground black pep
Celery leaves, to garn

Fall garni
1½ cups (150 g) fresh baby ceps, sli
3½ oz (100 g) raw duck foie gras, in pie
3½ oz (100 g) multicolored cherry tomatoes, skin
1 russet apple, quarte
1 stalk (50 g) celery, peeled and sli
3½ oz (100 g) fennel bulb, peeled and sli
8 fresh walnuts, shelled and pee
3 small red onions, sli
3½ oz (100 g) muscatel rais

Honey vineg
3 tablespoons (50 ml) walnut
3 tablespoons (50 ml) grapeseed
1¼ cups (30 ml) cider vine
1 teaspoon ho
Salt and pep

1
Spicy eggplant caviar

Preheat the oven to 325°F (160°C). Wash two of the Slim Jim eggplant and cut off the stalks. Stick the garlic cloves into them. Arrange the eggplant in a roasting pan and sprinkle with 2 tablespoons olive oil. Bake for around 1 hour. At the end of the cooking time, slice the eggplant in half lengthwise and scoop out the pulp and the garlic. Chop the garlic finely and reserve. Transfer the eggplant pulp to a saucepan and stir it constantly until it is a thick paste, as for choux pastry. Add a pinch of curry powder, the fresh thyme, minced garlic, lemon juice, and 4 tablespoons olive oil. Reserve at room temperature.

2

Prepare the fall garnish and reserve. Slice the mini-eggplants into thin slices. Heat the remaining olive oil in a frying pan and fry the eggplant. Reserve. Cut 4 thick slices from the remaining Slim Jim eggplants, sprinkle them with flour, and sauté them. Sprinkle with salt. Use two spoons to form two scoops of eggplant caviar and place them on each fried eggplant slice. Arrange the fall garnish around them.

3
Assembling the dish

Combine all the ingredients for the honey vinegar. To complete the dish, sprinkle it with a few drops of the honey vinegar and a few yellow celery leaves, some sea salt, and freshly ground black pepper.

Recommended wine: "L'atypique," Dry Bergerac 2003, Château Les Hauts-Caillevel, Sylvie Ducroq.

Slice of SLIM JIM EGGPLANT **with fall flavors**

SWEET CHERRY
PEPPER

by Joël

The sweet pepper I would need an entire book just to tell the story of peppers such as the pimento, bell, or chili pepper, and the innumerable varieties that exist throughout the world. The pepper is another member of the huge Solanaceae family, a cousin of the tomato, the eggplant, and the potato. The pepper comes to us from central America, at least in the case of the cultivated species. It was brought to Spain and propagated by the Franciscan monks, where it flourished in the monastery gardens. These monasteries also served as wayside stopping-places for the explorers who traveled throughout Europe, Africa, and Asia.

The term "bell pepper" or "sweet pepper" is used to describe the large, mild varieties, some of which—though not all—are oblong, others being pointed or round like a chili pepper. Calimero is a good example of a mild French pepper that looks like a chili. The fruit is dark green and globular like a small tomato. The flesh is solid and, upon ripening, turns deep red. In summer, it finds its place on our plates among the mini-zucchinis, mini-eggplant, baby pattypan squash, and other miniature vegetables.

Asia soon became the world's major producer and consumer of peppers. The chili is present in all the local cuisines and has become indispensable for the well-being of the local inhabitants. Meanwhile, in Paris, ANTOINE HEERAH, chef and owner of the restaurant LE CHAMARRÉ, has created one of his exciting recipes especially for this book. His cuisine lies mid-way between French and Asian cooking; Antoine comes from Mauritius, and so he quite naturally uses lots of peppers in his cooking. His know-how has enabled him not only to educate our European palates, but also to lead us among the subtle fragrances and flavors that magically transport us far away from our more familiar dishes.

SWEET CHERRY

by Antoine Heerah

PEPPER

Serves 4

Thick red snapper steak
12 x 4 oz (120 g) thick red snapper steaks
36 jumbo shrimp tails
½ teaspoon (3 g) table salt
¼ cup (50 ml) olive oil

Mango chutney with saffron
7 oz (200 g) semi-ripe, firm mango, julienned
¼ teaspoon (2 g) table salt
2 teaspoons (10 ml) cane sugar syrup
Juice of ½ lime
½ capsule powdered saffron
1 teaspoon (5 g) chopped garlic
10 drops green Tabasco sauce
4 teaspoons (20 ml) grapeseed oil

Red chili pepper chutney
7 oz (200 g) red chili pepper, seeded and thinly sliced
½ teaspoon (3 g) table salt
2 teaspoons (10 ml) cane syrup
Juice of ½ lime
4 teaspoons (20 g) chopped ginger root
5 drops green Tabasco sauce
4 teaspoons (20 ml) grapeseed oil

Sweet cherry pepper sauce
7 oz (200 g) sweet cherry pepper, seeded and chopped
1¾ oz (50 g) unsalted butter
1¾ oz (50 g) sorrel
⅓ cup (100 ml) light cream
Zest of ¼ kaffir lime
⅓ teaspoon (2 g) table salt
2 teaspoons (10 ml) cane syrup
1 scant cup (200 ml) shrimp cooking liquid
1 oz (30 g) flat-leaf parsley purée
½ lime, juice squeezed
15 drops green Tabasco sauce

1
Mango chutney with saffron
Season the julienned mango and macerate with the salt, cane sugar syrup, and lime juice for 30 minutes. Drain—reserving the liquid—and pat dry with absorbent paper. Add the saffron to the liquid and reduce. When it has almost dried up, remove it from the heat and add the garlic. Bind with the mango, grapeseed oil, and green Tabasco sauce. Reserve.

2
Red chili pepper chutney
Blanch the red chili pepper three times in cold water, bringing it to just below the boil. Refresh and drain. Season with salt, cane sugar syrup, and lime juice, and leave for 1 hour. Drain, reserving the liquid. Gently dry with absorbent paper. Reduce the juice until it has almost dried up. Remove from the heat and bind with the red chili pepper, ginger, Tabasco sauce, and grapeseed oil. Reserve.

3
Sweet cherry pepper sauce
Blanch the green pepper three times in cold water, bringing it to just below the boil. Refresh and drain. Heat the butter and cook the pepper on low heat with the sorrel, cream, kaffir lime zest, salt, and cane syrup. Cover and simmer for 90 minutes. Grind in a food processor while still hot with the shrimp cooking liquid and parsley purée. Strain and season with the lime juice and green Tabasco.

4
Finishing and assembling the dish
Season the red snapper and shrimp with salt. Heat the oil in a frying pan and sauté the shrimp for 30 seconds. Drain and replace with the fish: cook for 1 minute on each side. Arrange the mango chutney on one half of each red snapper slice and the red chili pepper chutney on the other. Sprinkle with olive oil and bake at 190°F (90°C) for 8 to 10 minutes, depending on thickness. Serve with the sweet pepper sauce and the shrimp.

Recommended wine: Côtes-de-Provence Blanc, Lady Jane 2002, Château Miraval.

Red snapper with Madras colors, mango chutney with saffron and
SWEET CHERRY PEPPER sauce

CANTALOUPE MELON

by Joël

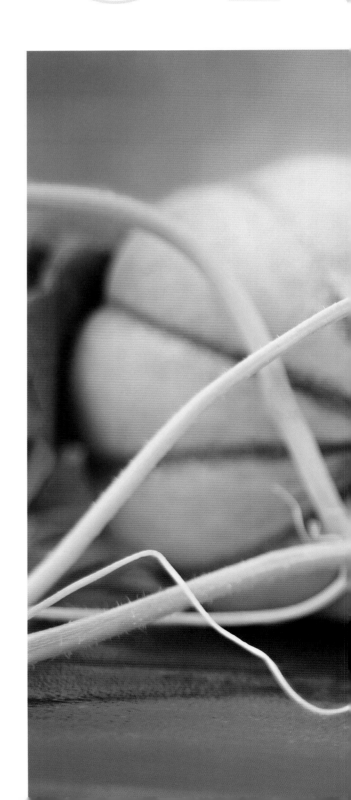

Cantaloupe melon

This fruit is of African origin: the most ancient traces of its cultivation are to be found in the Nile Valley. The melon is the quintessential symbol of summer and warmth. Its image as a southern plant is so intrinsic that one forgets that melons have been grown for centuries in the Île-de-France. Today, the melon varieties cultivated in the Paris region are of the Cantaloupe type, introduced into France during the Renaissance by Charles VIII, who brought them from Italy. In fact, the name Cantaloupe comes from "Cantalupo," the papal residence near Rome, to which this fruit had been brought from Armenia shortly before. Even though there was no talk of globalization in those days, food and seeds often migrated with greater ease than today. The melon that has been most frequently cultivated in France over the last fifty years has been the Charentais Cantaloupe. The reason it has come to represent a benchmark for melons is certainly in part because of its early ripening, since it develops only a month after fertilization, but also due to its wonderful eating qualities: it is fragrant and full of sweetness (saccharose) and has a luscious flesh. It may seem a paradox to include melon fruits in a book dedicated to varieties of vegetables, but melons are used as fruits almost exclusively in Europe produce: in the Far East and Africa they are often picked before they are ripe and eaten in salads, cooked or preserved. To maintain the paradox, I chose as the chef for this summer vegetable CHARLOTTE CHRISTIANSSON, a young woman who comes from Sweden. Charlotte is an expert in home cooking and her dynamism and passion for our vegetables is evident in her recipe.

CANTALOUPE
by Charlotte Christiansson
MELON

Serves 4

Melon granita
1 Cantaloupe melon
Juice of ½ lemon
1 tablespoon sugar
1½ tablespoons vodka

Serves 4

Mini-pizzas with melon and goat's cheese
1 tablespoon (15 g) fresh yeast
1 tablespoon sugar
1 scant cup (215 ml) lukewarm water
3 tablespoons olive oil
½ tablespoon salt
4 cups (450 g) all-purpose flour
½ Cantaloupe melon, thinly sliced
Goat's cheese, thinly sliced (do not use cheese that is too fresh)
Black pepper
A few mint leaves, finely chopped

Melon granita

1

Blend the granita ingredients for 2 minutes in a blender or food processor. Pour into a Tupperware and leave in the freezer for 3 hours.

2

Stir with a fork every 30 minutes. To serve, scrape the surface with a fork and serve in 4 glasses.

Mini-pizzas with Melon and Goat's Cheese

1

Dissolve the yeast and sugar in the warm water. Add the oil, salt, and flour and leave in a warm place for 1 hour. Knead the dough until smooth and no longer sticky, adding a little more flour if necessary. Roll out the dough until it is only ⅛ inch (2 mm) thick.

2

Cut out little rounds with a cookie cutter. Cover a cookie sheet with nonstick baking paper and place the rounds on it. Arrange slices of melon and goat's cheese alternately on the dough. Sprinkle with a few drops of olive oil and pepper. Bake at 400°F (200°C) for 10 to 15 minutes.

3

On removal from the oven, sprinkle the mini-pizzas with chopped mint and a little olive oil.

Recommended wine: Coteaux-du-layon.

CANTALOUPE MELON **granita and mini-pizzas with melon and goat's cheese**

BORAGE FLOWER

by Joël

Borage flower The survival instinct of the species is strongly developed in most of the plants that we grow and tend in our truck farms. But there is one that is particularly aggressive, with an acerbic character. That plant is borage. The plant that is sometimes known as the "vegetable oyster" seeds itself by wind and tide, and can easily run rampant. Whether blue or white, its fertilized flowers produce seeds that germinate rapidly. The young plants, with their slightly velvety leaves, are gathered early in the morning and brought to the kitchen immediately. There, they are worked to make them supple and pleasant to the taste. The stems appear very quickly. They are covered with pretty flowers that have a refreshing fragrance, slightly reminiscent of iodine, and enhance hot dishes and salads alike.

This plant—one of the most extraordinary in the garden—which adapts itself to every situation without being adversely affected by it, calls for a chef who practices his art in the same spirit: someone without preconceptions, who lets himself be led by the season, who is ready to create unexpected combinations, and who is capable of producing a dozen dishes in the shortest space of time. This phenomenon can only be IÑAKI AIZPITARTE.

BORAGE FLOWER
by Iñaki Aizpitarte

1

Cook the whelks in plenty of water with the bouquet garni for 30 to 40 minutes, depending on size.

2

Cut out the lettuce hearts and slice them in half lengthwise.

3

Shuck the oysters over a large bowl to collect the liquid. Put the oysters aside for the apéritif Add the lime juice to the liquid to season it, and strain.

4

Arrange the remaining ingredients, including the sprigs of borage flowers, decoratively and appetizingly in the bottom of a large burgundy glass, brandy snifter, or miniature goldfish bowl. Pour in enough of the seasoned oyster liquid to come half-way up the glass.

Recommended wine: Viognier, Harvests from the Domaine Rougier, Emmanuel de Sous at Rieux.

Serves 4

2 oz (50 g) whelks
1 bouquet garni
2 romaine lettuces
12 Cap-Ferret oysters
Juice of 1 lime
4 or 5 sprigs of borage flowers
1 oz (30 g) cooked bay shrimp
1½ oz (40 g) cooked cockles

Cockles, whelks, bay shrimp, and BORAGE FLOWERS **as if in an aquarium**

PURPLE GRAFFITI
CAULIFLOWER

by Joël

Purple cauliflower This variety, called Graffiti, is a descendant of the black and purple cauliflowers of Sicily. It is remarkable not only for the violet color of the flower, but also for its texture, which is denser than its white-flowered cousins. I have been growing these cauliflowers for several years, in the company of the Alverda and Romanesco cauliflower varieties, also originally from Italy but yellow and pale green respectively. Although all these colored variations are less easy to grow than the white ones, and consequently less productive, I think it is interesting to offer this kind of range, as it contributes to the richness of our cuisine. Perhaps my only regret is that some of the color is lost in cooking. That is because the anthocyanic pigments responsible for the coloring are water-soluble, so they dissolve during cooking. That is one of the reasons why the raw flower is sometimes scraped off and used raw as a sprinkle. The flavor and texture develop quickly at maturity, but can vary from one plant to the next. For such a rare plant, I could only call on a master of improvisation such as PIERRE GAGNAIRE, who always knows how to rise to the occasion irrespective of the produce on offer. Thanks to his fertile imagination, he is capable of transforming Graffiti into a genuine work of art.

PURPLE GRAFFIT
by Pierre Gagnaire
CAULIFLOWER

1

Cook two eggs at 145°F (63°C) for 90 minutes. Peel them and separate the whites from the yolks. Cut the cauliflower into four and cook it in slightly salted boiling water. Make sure it is cooked only until it is crunchy, so that the color remains strong and deep. Drain and rinse it under cold water.

2

Reduce the flavored cream over medium heat until it thickens, then salt it lightly. Leave to cool then incorporate the egg whites and chives. Grind the mixture in a food processor. Leave at room temperature.

3

Citrus syrup

Bring the grapefruit and lime juice to the boil and incorporate the softened gelatin. Add the herbs and long pepper and leave to infuse, then strain the mixture without pressing down. Blend the mixture in a blender to emulsify and refrigerate until required.

4

Mash the egg yolk with a little olive oil to make it smooth. Salt it lightly.

5

Assembling the dish

In a shallow bowl, place the mashed egg yolk and arrange the violet cauliflower quarters on top with the cream mixture and citrus syrup on the side. To garnish, sprinkle with the lime zest and add a few grains of salt coated in olive oil.

Recommended wine: Amontillado Seco Napoléon sherry, Bodega Hidalgo.

Serves 4

2 eggs
1 purple cauliflower
2 cups (500 ml) heavy cream with a little anise and 4 kaffir lime leaves
1 small bunch chives, chopped

Citrus syrup
2 cups (500 ml) pink grapefruit juice
Juice and zest of 2 limes
5 gelatin leaves, softened
1 bunch peppermint, verbena, and fresh coriander leaves
1 cubeb (long pepper)

Slices of PURPLE CAULIFLOWER, **with Hervé's egg, citrus syrup, fresh herbs and cubeb**

BABY
by Joël
BROAD BEAN

Baby broad bean I discovered how to grow this ancient vegetable only ten years or so ago. In particular, the variety Stereo, the very model of a new species that my chef friends, professional and amateur, all ask for. Some of them find in it the qualities of the beans they ate in childhood! That is impossible, because in these cases there are so many feelings and situations that are closely bound up with grandmother—who may now be long since passed away—and her famous beans that a humble grower such as myself could never hope to reproduce. In the Île-de-France, broad beans can be sown in the fall and spring and the harvest lasts from May through mid-July. You can even occasionally sow the beans in July with the intention of picking them in September, so long as the weather doesn't get too hot. Too much heat prevents the fertilization of the numerous white flowers, which blossom on stems that can grow as high as 4 feet (1.2 m). The Stereo bean is harvested when the pods are still light and contain beans the size of a pea. At this stage, you don't have to peel the bean twice, as the skin protecting the bean itself is thin and sweet; it is only as it ripens that the skin becomes slightly bitter and inedible and needs to be removed. When immature, the Stereo is remarkable for its powerful floral fragrance. Those lucky enough to taste this baby bean find themselves transported into an orangery in bloom. That is why it required the feminine sensibility of FLORA MIKULA, chef at her restaurant FLORA in Paris—as well as the spirit of her cooking, which deliberately looks to the south for inspiration—to turn this fine, precious seed into something sublime.

BABY
by Flora Mikula
BROAD BEAN

1

Milk shake (prepare the day before)
Blanch the beans in salted water for 5 minutes. Transfer to iced water to cool, then drain them. In a food processor, combine the pods, milk, coconut milk, and yogurt. Season and strain through a conical sieve. Refrigerate for at least 24 hours.

2

Humus (prepare the day before)
Blanch the shelled beans in salted water. Reserve them. Put the beans in their pods in a shallow saucepan, add the olive oil, salt and a little thyme. Cook on low heat for 30 minutes. Leave to cool in the oil. Drain, reserving the olive oil. Shell the beans and discard the pods.

In a food processor, grind the cooked beans and blanched beans. Add a little water to help the mixing. Combine it with the tahini and add a little olive oil and lemon juice. Season with salt and a pinch of red chili pepper. It should have the consistency of a paste. Refrigerate overnight.

3

Assembling the dish
Serve the milk shake in a long glass with a straw. Serve the humus next to it, accompanied by shrimp crackers or toast.

Recommended wine: Boulaouane Gris.

Serves 4

Milk shake
1 lb 2 oz (500 g) baby broad beans in the pod
3 cups (750 ml) milk
1 cup (250 ml) coconut milk
1 cup (250 ml) plain yogurt
Salt

Humus
3½ oz (100 g) shelled baby broad beans
10½ oz (300 g) baby broad beans in the pod
1 cup (250 ml) olive oil and a little water
Salt
1 sprig fresh thyme
1 large tablespoon tahina
Juice of 1 lemon
I pinch red chili pepper

To serve
Shrimp crackers or toast

BABY
BROAD
BEAN
**humus with
milk shake**

PURPLE ONION

by Joël

Purple onion You cannot pass by without noticing it, and at first glance you will be entranced by its flawless, shiny, dark-purple skin. I discovered it four years ago by accident, during one of my varietal trials. Since the 1980s I had been looking for a dark red onion that could be sown in spring and had a very mild flavor. Each time, the search was in vain. I would often find myself with a small onion that was very strongly flavored, especially if the summer had been cool. Imagine my surprise when I dared to taste this young bulb that had only just "turned," i.e, that had just passed the "crayon" stage. Each of the leaf wrappings that make up the onion is itself covered with a purplish-red skin on the outer surface. When cutting through the stem lengthwise, a section of purple stripes interspersed with white is revealed. At this stage, the little scallion has much the same smell and taste as a white onion—one that is very pleasant. It is even comparable to certain varieties of shallot, in that the flavor remains in the mouth for a long time. The most exciting part of this discovery is recognizing that I still have a lot to learn about this onion, which retains a multitude of secrets that are yet to be revealed. But aren't patience and perseverance the prime qualities that a vegetable-grower needs to possess?

Such a vegetable deserves to be placed in good hands; in this case they are those of JEAN-LUC POUJAURAN, a master baker who displays both respect for and understanding of the work of a grower. Here, he has combined the purple onion with a black tomato to make a most unusual and very subtle bread.

PURPLE ONION

by Jean-Luc Poujauran

1

The day before

Slice the tomatoes thinly and leave to dry on a rack in a dry place, or in an oven on its lowest setting (or with just the pilot light on) for 1 hour. Peel and slice the purple onions and fry them in a frying pan in a little olive oil. They should have just turned transparent and not be too well done. Reserve for the next day.

2

Dissolve the yeast in water in a warmed bowl. Add the flour and begin kneading by hand or with a dough hook until the dough is smooth and comes away from the sides of the bowl.

3

Incorporate the salt, onions, and dried tomato. Cover with a cloth and leave for 1 hour at room temperature.

4

Punch down the dough, shape it, and place it in a lightly oiled metal loaf pan or Pyrex dish.
Leave to rise for around 90 minutes, then bake in a preheated 475°F (250°C) oven for 50 minutes, placing a little bowl of water on the floor of the oven to keep the air moist.

5

Unmold the loaf and eat when cool.

Recommended wine: "Les Sorcières du Clos des Fées," Claudine and Hervé Bizeul, Vingrau.

Serves 4

8 oz (250 g) black tomatoes
7 oz (200 g) purple onions
Olive oil
4 teaspoons (20 g) fresh yeast
2¾ cups (650 ml) mineral water
9 cups (1 kg) strong white flour (type 70)
2 tablespoons salt

My black tomato and PURPLE ONION **bread**

SWEET WHITE ONION

by Joël

Sweet white onion I grow Wolf sweet onions, which, planted as the days shorten in the fall, only live in packs! Stretching out in rows up to 200 yards long, they are planted fairly close together, but not too much so or they risk overcrowding. The bulbs lie in wait all winter, until the spring thaw begins; they are able to withstand temperatures as low as 14°F (-10°C), though not for very long. If a cold snap lasts for several weeks, it will destroy them—or at best, many of the bulbs will run to seed, which will make them unusable anyway. As soon as the weather turns fine, the onion roots will run deep into the earth to find the energy they need for their development. If they are to reach full maturity, they need to be able to resist the violent rainstorms of May that sometimes turn to hail, as well as attacks by plant diseases and pests such as mildew or thrips. Then, in June, those golden bulbs with their very thin skin can finally be harvested. They are pulled out of the ground and left out for several days to dry, then gathered and stored in a cool, dry place. After trimming, they are gradually sold as needed, right up to Christmastime. By the time they are harvested, these wolves have turned into lambs! This is when their flesh is at its most luscious and tender, and their flavor is very sweet and mild. Gourmets use them raw or cooked, and they can be made into onion preserves.

My friend ÉRIC ROUX, a food writer and journalist and a broadcaster on food and cookery, never tires of searching for exceptional produce. He is also a passionate gardener in his native Auvergne, and a brilliant cook who has reworked the traditional pissaladière recipe just for us.

SWEET WHITE ONION

by Éric Roux

1
Anchovy sauce

Peel and slice one of the onions and the garlic cloves. In a small saucepan, cook them gently in the olive oil. Moisten with the lemon juice and cook until the liquid evaporates. Remove the bones from the salt anchovies and rinse them under the cold tap to remove the excess salt. Remove the saucepan from the heat and add the anchovies. Chop the feta cheese and add it. Process the mixture in a food processor until it sticks together. Reserve at room temperature.

2
Onion filling

Wash the remaining onions well and cut them into quarters. In a nonstick skillet, dry-fry them on each side. Place them on a sheet of aluminum foil large enough to wrap around them. Sprinkle with thyme, chili pepper, salt, and a teaspoon of olive oil. Seal them hermetically in the aluminum foil, ensuring they are loosely wrapped. Bake in a preheated oven at 275°F (140°C) for 1 hour.

3
Baking the dough

Roll out the dough as thinly as possible and cut out 8 strips, 1³⁄₄ inches x 8 inches (4 cm x 20 cm). Preheat the oven to 475°F (240°C). Arrange the strips on nonstick baking paper or a silicone baking sheet. Brush some of the anchovy sauce on the sides of the strips. Bake for a few minutes, until golden. Remove from the oven and reserve.

4
Assembling the dish

Remove the outer skin from the quartered onions. Divide the quartered onions between the strips of pastry. Slice the anchovies lengthwise and arrange them with the olives on each strip of pastry. Sprinkle with the anchovy sauce and arrange the hyssop flowers on top. Snip the green parts of the scallions on the diagonal and arrange them on the pastry as well.

Éric's tip

You can always add long strings of lemon zest, simmered for 1 hour on a low heat in 2 cups (500 ml) of water, with a tablespoon of sugar and a teaspoon of salt.

Recommended wine : Vieilles Vignes, Domaine de Peyra, Stéphane Majeune, Saint-Georges-sur-Allier.

Serves 4

9 medium sweet white onions
3 garlic cloves
3½ fl oz (100 ml) olive oil
Juice of ½ lemon
8 salt anchovies
2 oz (50 g) feta cheese
1 sprig thyme
Birdseye chili peppers
Salt
8 oz (250 g) bread dough or
pre-rolled pizza dough
12 green olives
Hyssop or thyme flowers
Scallions, green parts only

SWEET WHITE ONIONS **in a pissaladière**

CURRANT TOMATO
by Joël

Currant tomato This variety is called Mirabelle, and what could be more natural for this tiny fruit—so often considered to be a vegetable—than to take the name of a French variety of plum? Its tiny size and golden robe, which at the moment of picking is coated with a delicate bloom, means that it is entirely reminiscent of the Mirabelle plum variety. These tomatoes are to be found every morning in the market at my stand in a large wicker basket (they don't like plastic). Each is distinguished from its neighbor by its color, of course, as well as by the texture of the flesh, which may be juicy, luscious, and even faintly woolly, and then by the skin, which is thin but sometimes resistant to the teeth, and finally by its flavor, which may be very sweet or slightly acidic. The shape and size of these tomatoes have been described as "cherry, plum, or pear" and they are often eaten as fruits, either raw or cooked.

To amuse ourselves with these little "tidbits," and to make our mouths water with a dish that can be served as an appetizer or a dessert, we must turn to a great gourmet such as my friend BRUNO VERJUS. He is a great discoverer of unusually fine produce, one of the most talented of amateur cooks. He created this dish especially for us.

CURRANT TOMATO
by Bruno Verjus

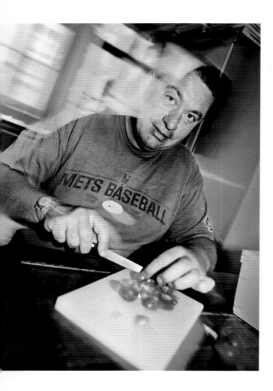

1

Shortcrust dough (prepare the day before)

Sift the flour into a bowl. Combine the salt and sugar with the milk. Put the softened butter into the bowl of a food processor. Beat on medium speed to soften and homogenize the butter, then add the mixture of milk, salt, and sugar. When the mixture is smooth and creamy, add the egg, then the flour.

As soon as the dough coheres into a ball, stop processing it immediately, or the texture will be spoiled. Roll it out into a round of 4 inches (10 cm) in diameter and cover with plastic wrap. Reserve in a cool place overnight.

(You can keep the dough for 48 hours in the refrigerator, or even freeze it.)

2

Roll out the dough in a rectangle to a thickness of ⅛ inch (3 mm). Grease and flour a cookie sheet. Lift the dough on a rolling pin and deposit it gently on the cookie sheet. Place rectangular molds (4 x 1⅝ inches [10 x 4 cm]) on the dough and use them like cookie cutters to cut out the base of the tarts. Make 8 or 10 in case any of them break. Discard the surplus dough around the cutouts. Refrigerate the cutouts for 1 hour.

3

Prick the cutout dough with the tines of a fork and carefully separate the rectangles from each other. Slide the tartlets into a preheated 370°F (180°C) oven and bake blind for 15 minutes.

4

Cut off a quarter of the vanilla bean (pod). Split it in two lengthwise and remove the seeds with a knife point. Place half the seeds in a small bowl with a little olive oil. Cover with plastic wrap and reserve at room temperature.

5

Melt the butter and quickly sauté the tomatoes (reserving the 12 with husks as well as a few small tomatoes to garnish) with a few of the remaining vanilla seeds. Fry the tomatoes only long enough for them to slightly soften and become coated in butter. Cover with plastic wrap and reserve at room temperature.

6

Remove the baked pastry rectangles from the oven and let them rest on the cookie sheet for a few minutes.

7

Bring a large pot of water to the boil and blanch the 12 tomatoes still attached to their husks. Cool immediately in an aluminum bowl filled with ice water. Skin the lower half of the tomatoes and pull up the upper part toward the husk, like a skirt raised by the wind.

8

On large white plates, place a rectangle of chilled burrata cheese at least 1⅝ inches (4 cm) thick. To do this, cut it out or mold it using the same rectangular molds that were used to cut out the tart pastry bases. Brush the tops of the cheeses with the vanilla-flavored oil. This will cover the cheeses with a waterproof film, preventing them from turning the tartlet pastry soggy.

9

Place a tartlet pastry on each cheese rectangle. On the tartlet, arrange two rows of cooked tomatoes. Arrange on the plate some of the blanched, half-skinned and some of the reserved raw tomatoes. Season with a few drops of the vanilla oil and with one or two grains of salt to taste.

Recommended wine: Carco, Grotte di Sole, Antoine Arena.

Serv

Shortcr
dou
2 cups (250 g)
purpose fl
1 teaspoon (5 g)
2 tablespoons (
confectioner's su
4 tablespo
(50 ml)
¾ cup (190 g) softe
bu
Yolk of 1 large

1 Mexican or bour
vanilla bean (p
Oliv
¾ oz (20 g) bu
14 oz (400 g) curr
tomatoes, inclu
12 with hu
2 burrata chee
Sea

MIRABELLE TOMATOES, **burrata, and Mexican vanilla**

KING EDWARD
by Joël

King Edward potato From the Solanaceae family, I have picked the "Saint Bernard" because this simple tuber, still called "papa" today by the Andean Indians, has been the means of subsistence for a large part of humanity during periods of famine. It was cultivated long before the arrival of the Spaniards, and had spread down the entire Andes range by the time the Spaniards landed on the shores of South America. The conquistadors were more interested in the Inca gold than in the potato, which appears to have reached Spain only thirty years later. This complete food with a high energy value was easily grown in the Canary Islands. It also keeps well and is easily transported making it of huge strategic importance for the Spanish armies. As the potato continued to spread throughout the world, it became the miracle solution for feeding starving populations. But disaster struck throughout Europe in 1845, in the shape of *Phytophthora infestans*: the Potato Blight. The fight against this fungal disease and its new mutations continues to this day. One of the ways to help prevent the propagation of blight consists in planting a wide number of varieties which will be genetically different from each other. That is what I do at my truck farm, growing ten or more varieties each year. They include an English "grandad" who is more than a hundred years old: the King Edward. This was the most popular and heavily cultivated potato in Great Britain during the first half of the twentieth century. The skin is darkish yellow, enhanced by circular pink patches around the eyes which are the starting point for future sprouts. This explains the name *Oeil-de-perdrix* (Partridge Eye) given to the variety in France a few years after its introduction. Its eating quality explains its popularity, and it is fortunate that it has once again become possible to grow it alongside popular French varieties such as the Ratte and the Vitelotte. As in the case of the tomato, I am grateful to Patrick and Lyndsay Mikanowski for having described so much of the history of this tuber in their book, *Patate*. They demonstrated how versatile it was and how it was able to adapt to the climatic conditions of its adopted homelands. I therefore decided to hand over this seasoned traveler to PAUL PAIRET, a "traveling chef" whom I first met at CAFÉ MOSAÏC in Paris. He now exercises his talents far from his country of origin since he is now to be found at JADE ON 36TH, the restaurant of the Shangri-La Hotel in Shanghai. From there, he will give us a glimpse of the culinary resourcefulness of the "earth apple."

KING EDWARD
by Paul Pairet

Ketchup sorbet

1

Process all the ingredients in a food processor.

2

Stir in an ice-cream maker to obtain a soft sorbet.

Maxi-fry

1

Cooking the fries

Scrub the potatoes under running water to clean them completely. Put them in a pot that is just large enough to hold them snugly. Cover them with cold water to a depth of about 2 inches (5 cm) above the potatoes. Bring to the boil on low heat and cook at a slow boil, until the potatoes are completely cooked through. Drain them, discarding the water, but do not peel them. Grind them in a vegetable mill over the cooking pot, which should still be hot.

2

Molding

Spread out, tamp down, and smooth the hot potato mash immediately in a rectangular mold 10 inches x 8 inches (25 cm x 20 cm) to a thickness of about ¾ inch (2 cm).

Refrigerate the mixture for 3 hours so that the potato mash becomes smoother as it cools and forms a compact mass with a thin crust on the surface. After this time, use a ruler and a cutter to cut out 4 fries ⅝ inch (1.5 cm) thick and about 8 inches (20 cm) long.

3

Drying the fries

Distribute the fries on a tray or cookie sheet, spacing them out and laying them on their upper surface (on which a crust formed when the mash was refrigerated), so that a crust is able to form on the other surfaces. Refrigerate, uncovered, at least overnight. (The drying time is long, but also depends on the variety and maturity of the potatoes used).

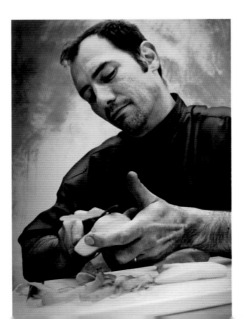

4

Finishing the dish

Heat the oil in a deep-fryer to 360°F (180°C) and proceed in two stages: Firstly, deep-fry the fries individually in the frying oil at 360°F (180°C) for about 5 minutes, or until they are slightly golden. Secondly, just before serving, fry the 4 fries together for 2 minutes—they should turn a beautiful golden color. Drain and pat dry on a double thickness of absorbent paper. Use a pastry brush to brush each fry on its upper side with a little truffle oil. Season generously with sea salt and coarsely ground black pepper.

Serve piping hot, with a large dab of ketchup sorbet.

Recommended wine: Côte-de-Beaune 2001, Lacimbe d'Ève, Domaine Emmanuel Giboulot.

Serves

Ketchup sorbe
1 cup (250 ml) ketch
⅖ cup (100 ml) warm wat
4 teaspoons (20 ml) balsamic vineg

Maxi-fr
2¼ lb (1 kg) floury potatoes of the bintje or King Edward ty
Oil for deep-fryi
Truffle
Sea salt and freshly ground black pepp

KING EDWARD **maxi-fry and ketchup sorbet**

HOKKAIDO SWEET SQUASH

by Joël

Hokkaido sweet squash This variety of squash comes from northern Japan, where it is also known as Chinese squash. In fact, it belongs to the North American group of cultivars known as Blue Hubbard squash. The squash reached Europe in the late 1950s but it has only been known to the general public for about twenty-five years. Its excellent reputation is due to its gustatory qualities, but its nutritional value puts it above many other vegetables. Although I am no expert in "nutraceuticals" and I mainly seek the best organoleptic qualities, I must mention in passing its richness in vitamins, trace elements, amino acids, natural sugars, and especially in carotene. On this last point, it is a true champion, containing twice as much provitamin A as carrots! What is also surprising about this squash is its very high density. It contains three times as much dry matter as most vegetables. In fact, when reduced to a purée, its flesh has a similar consistency to that of a chestnut. This "runner" squash is sown in early May, and extends its creepers over an area of about 10 feet (3 m) by the time it is fully grown. We put the fruit in a cool room (58°F/14°C) in October. Although the plant is relatively easy to grow, its storage is a fine art, requiring the skills of a specialist who can achieve the right temperature and humidity. A specialist has also been given the task of cooking this squash for us. JACQUES DECORET is the chef and owner of a restaurant of the same name in Vichy, where his fame has spread throughout the region. Assisted by his wife, Martine, who is also his ambassadress in the dining area, he has enabled the most daring, provocative, and distinctive cuisine in France to be accepted and even loved.

HOKKAIDO
by Jacques Decoret
SWEET SQUASH

1

Peel the squash and cut it into thin, regular slices. Put it into a pot of cold water and bring to the boil. Boil for 2 minutes just to blanch it.

2

Drain it, retaining 5 tablespoons (65 ml) of water. Cook the squash with the sugar, the reserved water, ginger, and split vanilla bean (pod). Leave to reduce and soften for about 1 hour.
Remove the vanilla and ginger, and chop the ginger finely.

3

Put the squash in a food processor and process so as to obtain a smooth paste. Incorporate the chopped ginger into it. Mold the paste into a hemisphere of about 1¾ (4 cm) inches in diameter and place it on the side of an egg dish.

4

Mix the cream cheese with the crème fraîche, whole milk, confectioner's sugar, and white rum. Pour it around the yellow squash "yolk."

5
Soldiers

Cut the rye bread into sticks ¾ inch (2 cm) wide. Cut the smoked bacon into equal-sized triangles. Sprinkle them on both sides with the confectioner's sugar. Toast the bread on one side and the bacon on both sides so that the bacon slightly caramelizes. Place the caramelized bacon on the toasted rye bread.

Serve the pretend egg accompanied by the "soldiers."

Recommended wine: Iced chestnut liqueur from the Jean Gauthier distillery at Saint-Désirat.

Serves

5½ oz (150 g) sweet squash
2 tablespoons (25 g) superfine sugar
½ slice ginger root
½ vanilla bean (pod)

5 teaspoons (50 g) smooth cream cheese
5 teaspoons (50 g) crème fraîche
5 teaspoons (50 ml) whole milk
2 tablespoons (15 g) confectioner's sugar
½ tablespoon white rum

Bread "soldiers"
1 thin slice smoked bacon
Confectioner's sugar
Rye bread

HOKKAIDO SWEET SQUASH **as a pretend egg**

PURPLE TOP
TURNIP

by Joël

The turnip

Since prehistoric times, and before it was supplanted by the potato, a root vegetable that was a distant ancestor of the modern turnip formed a staple of the human and animal diet. In the early nineteenth century, the vegetable growers of the Île-de-France began selecting the turnip varieties that were best suited to local growing conditions, such as the turnips of Meaux, Croissy, Vaugirard, Montmagny, and Fresneuse. Today, even though turnip consumption is relatively low, local growers are still teaching new generations about the subtlety of the fragrance and flavor of this plant and the range of its possibilities in cooking, where it can be used not just for its tap root, but also for its leaves and even its flowers.

Throughout the year, except possibly at the height of summer when the heat makes the flavor too strong and the flesh too fibrous, the turnip should have a place in your kitchen. In spring, you will find the little, flat, white tap roots with their violet ring round the top. This is the Milan turnip. Then there is the flat yellow Petrowski turnip or rutabaga. In fall and winter, the big, golden balls of rutabaga and the white Croissy turnip are popular in France, as is the round white Nancy turnip, with its purple collar, which is very similar to the variety Purple Top White Globe. The Nancy turnip is the one that I gave to ÉRIC FRECHON, the head chef at the famous HÔTEL BRISTOL in Paris. I knew that he would create a recipe that would show how this very ancient vegetable can become something exotic and exciting, making it as interesting as ever, fit for twenty-first century cuisine.

PURPLE TOP TURNIP

by Éric Frechon

Serves 4

1 cup (250 g) superfine sugar
5 tablespoons (50 ml) water
Zest of 1 untreated lemon
2 large purple top turnips
1 scant cup (200 g) butter
1 teaspoon honey
4¼ cups (1 l) orange juice
1¾ oz (50 g) ginger
1 sprig rosemary

1
Make a syrup by combining the sugar and water, and bring to the boil. Add the lemon zest and cook, covered, on a low heat for about 40 minutes. Drain, dry the lemon zests then chop finely. Reserve.

2
Peel and slice the turnips, then use a round cookie cutter about 2 in (5 cm) in diameter to cut out rounds. Fry the rounds in butter. Add the honey, deglaze with orange juice, and cook until soft.

3
Grate the ginger and chop the rosemary leaves. Sprinkle the turnips with the lemon zest, grated ginger, and chopped rosemary.

These rounds can be eaten as an appetizer or as a side dish.

Recommended wine: Condrieu "vendanges tardives" 2002, Domaine François Villard.

**Rounds of
TURNIP
with orange and
ginger**

JERUSALEM ARTICHOKE
by Joël

Jerusalem artichoke

For Frenchmen old enough to remember World War II, the Jerusalem artichoke may well evoke memories of a vegetable that was too often eaten back then to be of much interest today. For the younger generations, it is often considered an "old-fashioned vegetable" that has made a comeback after several decades of oblivion. Its late flowering and the way that the flower turns to the sun are reminders that the Jerusalem artichoke is a close relative of the sunflower. Its flavor is similar to that of the globe artichoke and both contain inulin, a valuable polysaccharide that is also found in dahlia tubers. The Jerusalem artichoke was discovered by the French explorer, Samuel de Champlain, on his second expedition to Canada in the early seventeenth century. It spread very quickly through France, but could not withstand the competition from the potato, which took hold in the following century. Only its ability to grow on poor and difficult soil saved it from total oblivion. Today, and for the past ten years, I have been growing the Jerusalem artichoke on the poorest quality and most pebbly soil on the truck farm—with good results nevertheless. When planted in mid-April, the plant sprouts rapidly, and the young shoots emerge from the soil, raising the earth that covers them. After a few weeks, they have grown into tall stems that will only flower in October, which is when I start to lift them. I just use a spade because the tubers are too fragile to be able to withstand mechanical harvesting. The Jerusalem artichoke is of great interest as a culinary vegetable because it is young and fresh in the fall rather than the spring, but its flavor does not fully mature until after the winter frosts. The irregular shape of the Jerusalem artichoke is the last sign of resistance when placed before ALEXANDRE MATHIEU, the generous and inventive chef and owner of the BISTRAL in Paris.

JERUSALEM ARTICHOKE
by Alex Mathieu & Thierry Berland

1

Olive ice cream (prepare the day before)
Beat the egg yolks with the sugar until light and fluffy. Heat the milk, citrus juice, and zest. Combine the egg yolk mixture with the citrus and cook in a double boiler to make a custard. When it is thick enough to coat the back of a spoon, leave it to cool, then add the cream and the olive paste. Process until smooth, then chill overnight in the refrigerator. Make the ice cream at the beginning of the meal, using a superfast ice-cream maker.

2

Preheat the oven to 450°F (230°C). Brush the rounds of flaky pastry dough with the egg yolk and place a rack 6 inches (15 cm) above the dough to ensure the pastry does not rise too high. Reduce the oven temperature to 360°F (180°C) and bake for 15 minutes.

3

Use a mandolin slicer to slice the unpeeled Jerusalem artichokes into pieces ⅛ inch (2–3 mm) thick. Make the poaching syrup by combining the water, sugar, lime juice, vanilla, and star anise. Add the Jerusalem artichokes and cook them. They should remain crunchy but cooked through. Leave them to cool in the syrup.

4

Aniseed-flavored dried fruit butter
Combine all the ingredients for the dried fruit butter in a bowl. Beat with a whisk to obtain a smooth paste.

5

Sweet potato filling with saffron
Peel the sweet potato and cut it into pieces. Add the butter, sugar, orange juice, and saffron to the water and cook the sweet potato in the liquid. When it is well cooked, drain it, and process it to make a smooth purée.

6

Place 1 tablespoon of the sweet potato filling on each round of the flaky pastry. Drain the Jerusalem artichoke slices and arrange them in overlapping slices in a rose shape on top of the sweet potato filling. Preheat the oven to 400°F (200°C). Put an equal amount of dried fruit butter on the top of each tart and bake for 5–10 minutes to cook the dried fruits and finish baking the pastry.

7
Milk shake
Meanwhile, heat the goat's milk, cow's milk, and sugar, and reduce by half. Cool, then refrigerate. Blend just before serving, so that it foams.

8

Arrange the flaky pastry tarts on serving plates when they come out of the oven. Pour a trickle of the foaming milk shake around each one, and add a scoop of olive ice cream. Decorate with star anise and a few saffron pistils.

Recommended wine: Les P'tites Bulles 2003, Pineau d'Aunis, Domaine Le Briseau (naturally sparkling).

Serve

Olive ice crea
6 egg yo
2¾ tablespoons (75 g) su
2 cups (500 ml) n
Juice & zest of ½ grapefr
Juice of ½ oran
Juice of ½ lem
1 cup (250 ml) heavy crea
½ cup (120 g) olive paste (tapena

Flaky pastry doug
Four 5-in (12-cm) diameter rounds of fl
pastry dough, ½ inch (1 cm) th
1 beaten egg yolk for glazi

8 large (2¼ lb/1 kg) Jerusal
artichokes, washed and scrubb

Poaching syru
4¼ cups (1 liter) wa
6 tablespoons (170 g) su
Juice of 4 lim
1 vanilla bean (pod), 2 star an

Aniseed-flavored dried fruit butt
1 cup (250 g) softened but
3 dried figs, chopp
5 dried apricots, chopp
1 tablespoon (15 g) almonds, blanched and sliver
1 tablespoon (15 g) hazelnuts, chopp
1 tablespoon (15 g) pistachios, chopp
1⅓ cups (150 g) confectioner's su
4 tablespoons (50 ml) pas
or aniseed-flavored liqu
2 pinches ground anise

Sweet potato filling with saffr
One 8-oz (250 g) sweet potato (yellow ya
4¼ cups (1 l) wa
4 tablespoons (50 g) but
2 tablespoons (50 g) su
Juice of 2 orang
2 pinches Spanish saffron stra

Milk sha
2 cups (500 ml) raw goat's m
2 cups (500 ml) raw whole cow's m
⅓ cup (100 g) su

Star anise and saffron pistils, to garn

JERUSALEM ARTICHOKE flaky pastry tart, with aniseed-flavored dried fruits,
sweet potato filling with saffron, goat's-milk milk shake, and olive ice cream

MONARCH
CELERY ROOT
by Joël

Monarch celery root

The celery root is a descendant of the wild or marsh celery (*Apium graveolens*), which was an important medicinal plant and was also used as a condiment. It was first bred as a root vegetable in Germany; the first variety to be mentioned was the Erfurt celery root in the sixteenth century. In France, it was only propagated in significant amounts after 1815. For a long time, the roots were very diverse in their shapes and textures, as well as in terms of the amount of time they could be kept. Modern selection techniques have enabled us to obtain more compact, less fibrous textures. I have been growing the Monarch variety for about fifteen years. By watching it and understanding how it develops, I have been able to offer a product that has improved from year to year. But there is no certainty when, in May, we plant out the seedlings propagated in the nursery. We need to ensure that the root system grows very slowly, as the tap root contains the plant's reserves and the leaf system is its lungs. We need to keep it vegetating but must not overwater it. The aim is to favor the enlargement of the taproot "ball" as late as possible—it should weigh 2¼ lb (1 kg) maximum. If all goes well, no black rot will develop in the center, and the center will remain solid, even in March after three months' preservation. The plant is harvested in November, before the sharp frosts, and the root is stored in the cold store in the same way as the beets.

So, celery root is a delicate plant that is unreliable and uninteresting if not carefully nurtured: a true truck farm vegetable, in fact! ALAIN PASSARD is a chef who knows it well. At his restaurant L'ARPÈGE, he has long understood that under this unrefined exterior there lies a fine, delicately flavored and powerful flesh. It is clear, when tasting his creations, that this "ball" has lost itself in his cooking only to reveal itself in all its glory.

MONARCH
CELERY ROOT
by Alain Passard

1

Cut off the bottom of the celery root to give a secure base and cut off the top. Scoop out the flesh with a teaspoon, leaving a ¹⁄₂ in (1 cm) thickness of flesh inside the root. Steam the removed flesh.

2

Grind the cooked flesh in a food processor, gradually adding the butter in pieces, the two egg yolks, the Orleans mustard, a pinch of grated nutmeg, and a pinch of sea salt.

3

Beat the egg whites into stiff peaks and use a wooden spoon to fold them into the celery mixture.

4

Pour the mixture back into the celery root shell and bake in a preheated 375°F (180°C) oven for 40 minutes. Sprinkle with minced parsley and serve immediately.

Recommended wine: Shoenenbourg Grand Cru 1999, Marcel Deiss.

Serves

1 Monarch celery root, weighing about 1 lb 2 oz (500 g)
2 tablespoons (30 g) unsalted butter
2 egg yolks
1 tablespoon Orleans mustard
Nutmeg
Sea salt
6 egg whites
1 tablespoon minced parsley

MONARCH CELERY ROOT **soufflé with Orleans mustard**

GUERNSEY PARSNIP

by Joël

Guernsey parsnip This vegetable has a rather primitive look about it, with its numerous rootlets. It is often confused with the white carrot. It appears to be coming back into fashion in France among chefs and amateur cooks alike.

I sow the small, flat seeds on my limestone soil in mid-June. They need to be sown soon after picking as they are viable for only a short time. The plant grows slowly, but once it has "taken" it is likely to flourish; it is tougher than its cousin the carrot, due to its ancient lineage. The thick, tough leaves are halfway between those of flat leaf parsley and celery. From the latter, it has inherited the luscious texture and silvery-white color of the flesh. It can survive the rigors of winter while in the ground, and it is thanks to the cold that the starch that has accumulated in the root during the summer is partly turned into sugar. The Semi-long Guernsey variety is a reminder that the English are particularly fond of the powerful, sweet taste of the parsnip. As avid consumers of the vegetable, they have even used the high carbohydrate content of the parsnip to turn it into parsnip wine, parsnip jam, and a sweet flour used in pastry making. So let us see what our favorite Breton chef, JEAN-MARIE BAUDIC of the restaurant AUX PESKED, a brilliant promoter of contemporary cuisine, has dreamed up for this root.

GUERNSEY PARSNIP
by Jean-Marie Baudic

1
Parsnip crunch

Peel and dice the parsnip. Pour the milk into a saucepan and add the parsnip. Bring to the boil, cover, and simmer for 30 minutes. Drain the parsnip, reserving the milk to make the ice cream and an emulsion (see steps 2 and 3). Process the parsnip in a food processor, adding the powdered cream and seasoning. Spread it out on a silicone baking sheet and bake for 6 minutes in a preheated 350°F (170°C) oven.

2
Parsnip ice cream

Mix 1 cup (250 ml) of the milk in which the parsnips were cooked with the egg yolks. Cook as a custard in a double boiler at 187°F (86°C) until the mixture coats the back of a spoon. Remove from the heat and stop the cooking by adding the heavy cream.
Incorporate the Trimoline or corn syrup and the stabilizer or cream of tartar when the mixture has cooled to 113°F (45°C). Process the mixture

obtained and rectify the seasoning if required. Pour into an ice-cream maker and make into ice cream. Place in the freezer.

3
Parsnip emulsion

Warm the rest of the parsnip cooking milk and dissolve the soy lecithin in it. Process in a food processor or blender and add a little hazelnut oil. Check the seasoning. Reheat, but do not let it boil.

4
Braised parsnip mille-feuille with Vadouvan spices and marinated tuna

Peel the parsnip and cut it into large sticks. Arrange the sticks on a cookie sheet. Sprinkle with the spice and the chicken broth. Bake in a preheated 350°F (170°C) oven for 1 hour, sprinkling and basting frequently with the broth.
Cut the tuna into sticks the same size as those of the parsnip and marinate them for 2 hours in the marinade.

5
Assembling the dish

Cut the parsnip and tuna into slices ⅛ inch (2 mm) thick, then use a deep hoop to arrange them in a mille-feuille.
Serve the mille-feuille at room temperature, with a scoop of ice cream stuck with 3 parsnip crunches, not forgetting to add a tablespoon of the parsnip emulsion.

Recommended wine: Muscadet Sèvre-et-Maine 2000, Marie-Luce Métaireau selection.

Serves 4

Parsnip crunch
8 oz (250 g) Guernsey parsnip
3 cups (750 ml) milk
2 tablespoons (25 g) powdered cream
Salt and pepper

Parsnip ice cream
1 cup (250 ml) of milk infused with parsnip (from the parsnip crunch recipe above)
1¾ oz (50 g) egg yolks
1 teaspoon (6 g) Trimoline or 1 teaspoon corn syrup
1 pinch (1 g) of stabilizer or cream of tartar
4 tablespoons (50 ml) heavy cream
Salt and pepper

Parsnip emulsion
1 teaspoon soy lecithin
Hazelnut oil

Braised parsnip mille-feuille with Vadouvan spice mixture
1 medium Guernsey parsnip
½ teaspoon Vadouvan spice mixture
1 cup (250 ml) chicken broth

Marinated tuna
1 thick slice red tuna
4 tablespoons (50 ml) olive oil
2 teaspoons (10 ml) soy sauce
½ teaspoon (2.5 g) grated ginger root
Salt, pepper, cayenne pepper
Zest of ½ lime

GUERNSEY PARSNIP: **not really forgotten**

FARMER JOËL

S NOTEBOOKS

USEFUL ADDRESSES of
CHEFS & FRIENDS OF JOË

Iñaki Aizpitarte, page 124
Le P'tit Mac (restaurant of the Musée d'Art
Contemporain, Vitry)
Impasse de la Libération,
94400 Vitry-sur-Seine
Tel: +33 (0)6 14 35 25 45

Frédéric Anton, page 48
Le Pré Catelan
Bois de Boulogne, Route de Suresnes,
75016 Paris
Tel: +33 (0)1 44 14 41 14
Website: www.lenotre.fr

Pascal Barbot, page 44
L'Astrance
4, Rue Beethoven, 75016 Paris
Tel : +33 (0)1 40 50 84 40

Jean-Marie Baudic, page 168
Aux Pesked
59, Rue du Légué, 22000 Saint-Brieuc
Tel: +33 (0)2 96 33 34 65
Email: jmbaudic@wanadoo.fr
Website: www.auxpesked.com

Éric Briffard, page 112
Les Élysées du Vernet
25, Rue Vernet, 75008 Paris
Tel: +33 (0)1 44 31 98 98
Email: elysees@hotelvernet.com
Website: www.hotelvernet.com

Raimundo Briones & Antoine Meyssonnier, page 88
Le Haut du Panier
25, Rue Jacques-Dulud,
92200 Neuilly-sur-Seine
Tel: +33 (0)1 47 47 61 15
Email: contact@lehautdupanier.com
Website: www.lehautdupanier.com

François Brouilly, page 28
Botanique Éditions
Lieu-dit Les Beurreries, 78810 Feucherolles
Tel: +33 (0)1 30 54 35 91
Website: www.botaniqueeditions.com

Raquel Carena, page 36
Le Baratin
3, Rue Jouye-Rouve, 75020 Paris
Tel: +33 (0)1 43 49 39 70

Charlotte Christiansson, page 120
La Cuisine de Charlotte
18, Rue du Bouquet-de-Longchamp,
75116 Paris
Tel: +33 (0)6 14 05 54 62
Email: svenskt@wanadoo.fr

Hélène Darroze, page 76
Hélène Darroze
4, Rue d'Assas, 75006 Paris
Tel: +33 (0)1 42 22 00 11
Email: reservation@helenedarroze.com
Website: www.helenedarroze.com

Jacques Decoret, page 152
Jacques Decoret
7, Avenue Gramont, 03200 Vichy
Tel: +33 (0)4 70 97 65 06
Email: jacques.decoret@wanadoo.fr
Website: www.jacquesdecoret.com

Éric Frechon, page 156
Le Bristol
112, Rue du Faubourg-Saint-Honoré,
75008 Paris
Tel: +33 (0)1 53 43 43 00
Website: www.hotel-bristol.com

Pierre Gagnaire, page 128
Pierre Gagnaire
6, Rue Balzac, 75008 Paris
Tel: +33 (0)1 58 36 12 50
Website: www.pierre-gagnaire.com

Catherine Guerraz, page 68
Chez Catherine
3, Rue Berryer, 75008 Paris
Tel: +33 (0)1 40 76 01 40

Benoît Guichard, page 40
Le Jamin
32, Rue de Longchamp, 75016 Paris
Tel: +33 (0)1 45 53 00 07
Email: reservation@jamin.fr

Olivier Guyon, page 80
Goumard
9, Rue Duphot, 75001 Paris
Tel: +33 (0)1 42 60 36 07
Email: olive.guyon@wanadoo.fr
Website: www.goumard.fr

Antoine Heerah, page 116
Le Chamarré
13, Boulevard La Tour-Maubourg, 75007 Paris
Tel: +33 (0)1 47 05 50 18
Email: chantallaval@wanadoo.fr

Pierre Hermé, page 100
Pierre Hermé
72, Rue Bonaparte, 75006 Paris
Tel: +33 (0)1 43 54 47 77
185, Rue de Vaugirard, 75015 Paris
Tel: +33 (0)1 43 54 89 96
In Japan: *Pierre Hermé Paris*
The New Otani, 4–1 Kioi-cho, Chiyoda-Ku,
Tokyo 102-8578. Tel: +81 (0)3 32 21 72 52
319, Ikspiari 1–4 Maihama, Urayasu-Shi,
Chiba-Ken 279-8529
Tel: +81 (0)4 73 05 56 55
La Porte Aoyama, 1F–2F - 5-51-8 Jingumae,

Shibuya-ku, Tokyo 150-0001
Tel: +81 (0)3 54 85 77 66
Website: www.pierreherme.com

Taïra Kurihara, page 108
Taïra
10, Rue des Acacias, 75017 Paris
Tel: +33 (0)1 47 66 74 14
Email: info@restaurant-taira.com
Website: www.restaurant-taira.com

William Ledeuil, page 104
Ze Kitchen Galerie
4, Rue des Grands-Augustins, 75006 Paris
Tel: +33 (0)1 44 32 00 32, fax : +33 (0)1 44 32 00 33
Website: www.zekitchengalerie.fr

Manuel Martinez, page 92
Relais Louis XIII
8, Rue des Grands-Augustins, 75006 Paris
Tel : +33 (0)1 43 26 75 96
Email: contact@relaislouis13.com
Website: www.relaislouis13.com

Alexandre Mathieu & Thierry Berland, page 160
Le Bistral
80, Rue Lemercier, 75017 Paris
Tel: +33 (0)1 42 63 59 61

Flora Mikula, page 132
Flora
36, Avenue George V, 75008 Paris
Tel: +33 (0)1 40 70 10 49
Email: raphael.restaurantflora@wanadoo.fr

Jean-Louis Nomicos, page 64
Restaurant Lasserre
17, Avenue Franklin D. Roosevelt, 75008 Paris
Tel: +33 (0)1 43 59 53 43
Email: lasserre@lasserre.fr

Paul Pairet, page 148
Jade on 36th (Pudong Shangri-La Hotel)
33 Fu Cheng Road, Pudong New Area,
Shanghai, China. Tel: +86 21 6882 8888
Email: paulpairet@mageos.com
Website: www.shangri-la.com

Alain Passard, page 164
L'Arpège
84, Rue de Varenne, 75007 Paris
Tel: +33 (0)1 45 51 47 33
Email: arpege.passard@wanadoo.fr
Website: www.alain-passard.com

USEFUL ADDRESSES FOR GARDENERS

Bibliography

Ford, Brian J. *The Future of Food.* New York: Thames & Hudson, 2000.

Jouan, Louis. *Histoire de Carrières-sur-Seine.* Carrières-sur-Seine: Municipality of Carrières-sur-Seine, 1978.

Larkcom, Joy. *The Organic Salad Garden.* London: Frances Lincoln, 2001.

Maincent-Morel, Michel. *La cuisine de référence, techniques et préparations de base, fiches techniques de fabrication.* Clichy: Éditions BPI, 2002.

Nestle, Marion. *Food Politics, How the Food Industry Influences Nutrition and Health.* Berkeley: University of California Press, 2002.

Nestle, Marion. *Safe Food, Bacteria, Biotechnology, and Bioterrorism.* Berkeley: University of California Press, 2003.

Pennaneac'h, Sandrine. *Carrières-sur-Seine, 2000 ans d'histoire, Vol. 1.* Published for the town of Carrières-sur-Seine/Soregraph, 2000.

Pitrat, Michel and Claude Foury, eds. *Histoires de légumes des origines à l'orée du XXIe siècle.* Paris, INRA, , 2003.

Schlosser, Eric. *Fast Food Nation, What the All-American Meal is Doing to the World.* London: Penguin Books, 2002.

Schneider, Elizabeth. *The Essential Reference, Vegetables from Amaranth to Zucchini.* New York: William Morrow, 2001.

Schneider, Elizabeth *Uncommon Fruits & Vegetables, A Commonsense Guide.* New York: William Morrow, 1998.

Viard, Michel. *Légumes d'autrefois.* Paris: Flammarion, 2005.

Senderens, Alain and Alain Weill, eds. *L'Inventaire du patrimoine culinaire de la France, Ile-de-France, Produits du terroir et recettes traditionnelles.* Paris: Albin Michel/CNAC, 1993.

Willemain, Daniel. "Histoire de l'agriculture, viticulture, maraîchage, myciculture et du syndicat agricole à Carrières-sur-Seine." Typewritten text.

UNITED KINGDOM

MEAT

Denhay Farms Ltd.
Broadoak, Bridport, Dorset DT6 5NP
Tel: +44 (0)1308 458963 / Fax: +44 (0)1308 424846
www.denhay.co.uk
Producers of air-dried ham, bacon, Dorset Drums (cheddar).

Donald Russell Direct
FREEPOST SCO 4131, Inverurie, Aberdeenshire, AB51 4ZL
Tel: +44 (0)1467 629666
www.donaldrusselldirect.com
Excellent Scottish butchers, whose truly wonderful meat is vacuum-packed so that it can be kept in the refrigerator for up to 3 weeks.

Lidgate Butchers
110 Holland Park Avenue, London W11 4UA
Tel: +44 (0)20 7727 8243
Specialize in naturally reared meats. They also sell a wide range of homemade sausages, quiches, and award-winning pies.

The Old Dairy Farm Shop
Path Hill Farm, Whitchurch on Thames, Berkshire RG8 7RE
Tel: +44 (0)118 984 2392
Organic meat, poultry, and eggs.

CHEESE

La Fromagerie
2–4 Moxon Street, London W1 4EW
Tel: +44 (0)20 7935 0341
and 30 Highbury Park, London N5 2AA
Tel: +44 (0)20 7359 7440
www.lafromagerie.co.uk
Italian, French, and British cheeses, as well as Poilâne bread, Venetian pasta, cakes, and more.

Neal's Yard Dairy
17 Shorts Gardens, London WC2H 9UP
Tel: +44 (0)20 7240 5700
and 6 Park Street, Borough Market, London SE1 9AB
Tel: +44 (0)20 7645 3554
www.nealsyarddairy.co.uk
Cheese from all over the British Isles.

GENERAL

The Real Food Store
14 Clifton Road, London W9 1SS
Tel: +44 (0)20 7266 1162

Selfridges Food Hall
400 Oxford Street, London W1A 1AB
Tel: +44 (0)8708 377 377
www.selfridges.co.uk

Villandry
170 Great Portland Street, London W1N 5TB
Tel: +44 (0)20 7631 3131
www.villandry.com

Planet Organic
25 Effie Road, London SW6 1EL
Tel: +44 (0)20 7731 7222
and 42 Westbourne Grove, London W2 5SH
Tel: +44 (0)20 7727 2227
and 22 Torrington Place, London WC1 7JE
Tel: +44 (0)20 7436 1929
www.planetorganic.com

Joubère
Freshly prepared stock—beef, lamb, chicken, veal, vegetable, game, and fish—of an incredibly high standard and sold in 300 ml tubs. Telephone +44 (0)20 8992 6851 for stockists.

The Oil Merchant
Tel: +44 (0)20 8740 1335
The_Oil_Merchant@compuserve.com
Olive, nut, and infused oils.

FISH

Cornish Fish Direct
The Pilchard Works, Newlyn, Penzance, Cornwall
Tel: +44 (0)1736 332112 / Fax: +44 (0)1736 332442
Overnight delivery of fresh Cornish fish.

G.B. Shellfish
Lochnell Estate, Benderloch, Argyll PA37 1QU
Tel: +44 (0)1631 720525
Scallops, mussels, oysters, etc., from the west coast of Scotland.

VEGETABLES

Jekka's Herb Farm
Tel: +44 (0)1454 418878
www.jekkasherbfarm.com / farm@jekkasherbfarm.com
Specializing in organic, culinary, aromatic, decorative, and medicinal herbs.

The Soil Association
40–56 Victoria Street, Bristol BS1 6BY
Tel: +44 (0)117 314 5000
info@soilassociation.org

Soil Association Scotland
18 Liberton Brae, Tower Mains, Edinburgh
EH16 6AE. Tel: +44 (0)131 666 2474
contact@sascotland.org
Contact the Soil Association for information on deliveries of organic vegetables in your area, or to order their full organic shopping catalog.

Sunnyfields Organic
Jacobs Gutter Lane, Totton, Southampton SO40 9FX
Tel: +44 (0)2380 861266 / Fax: +44 (0)2380 86124
Organic vegetables.

Further reading

Ducasse, Alain. Grand Livre de Cuisine: Alain Ducasse's Culinary Encyclopedia. New York, Harry Abrams, 2004.

Bacon, Josephine. Exotic Fruits and Vegetables, A–Z. St. Leonards: UPSO Publishing, 2005

Ledeuil, William. Les Couleurs du goût: la cuisine de William Ledeuil. Paris: Éditions du Seuil, 2004.

Mikanowski, Lyndsay and Patrick Mikanowski. Tomate. Paris: Éditions du Chêne, 2000.

Mikanowski, Lyndsay and Patrick Mikanowski. Patate. New York: Rizzoli, 2003.

Mikanowski, Lyndsay and Patrick Mikanowski. Uncooked. Paris: Flammarion, 2005.

Troisgros, Michel. La Cuisine acidulée de Michel Troisgros. Paris: Le Cherche Midi, 2004.

Joyce, Jennifer. The Well-dressed Salad: contemporary, delicious, and satisfying recipes for salads. New York: Whitecap Books, 2003.

Spieler, Marlena . The Vegetarian Bistro: 50 authentic French regional recipes. San Francisco: Chronicle Books, 1997.

Spieler, Marlena. Vegetable. San Francisco: Williams Sonoma, 2002.

Wright, Clifford. Mediterranean Vegetables: a cook's ABC of vegetables and their preparation. Boston: Harvard Common Press, 2001.

AUSTRALIA

New Gippsland Seeds & Bulbs
PO Box 1, Silvan, Victoria 3795
Tel: 03-9737 9560 / Fax: 03 9737 9292
Vegetable and herb seeds. Many old and unusual varieties.

Herbs & Cottage Plants Nursery
942 Main Road, Hurstbridge, Melbourne, Victoria 3099
Tel: (03) 9718 2249 / Fax: (03) 9439 5121
torkkola@smart.net.au
Bushfood plants, native and exotic herbs. Specialist retail nursery and mail order.

Eden Seeds
M.S. 316, 21a Sandy Creek Road, Gympie, Queensland 4570
Tel/fax: 1800 188 199
Organic vegetable seeds. Mail order and catalog.

Seed Savers' Network
P.O. Box 975, Byron Bay, NSW 2481
Tel: +61 02 6685 6624 / Fax: +61 02 6685 7560
www.seedsavers.net / info@seedsavers.net
Seed exchange organization that aims to conserve local and traditional varieties of vegetables, fruit, and other plants.

NORTH AMERICA

Baker Creek Heirloom Seeds
2278 Baker Creek Road, Mansfield, MO 65704
(417) 924-8917
www.rareseeds.com
Catalog offers more than 500 non-hybrid vegetables, flowers, and herbs.

W. Altee Burpee Company
300 Park Avenue, Warminster, PA 18974
(800) 333-5808
www.burpee.com
Catalog offers a nice selection of heirloom vegetable seeds.

Heirloom Seed Project
Landis Valley Museum
2451 Kissel Hill Road, Lancaster, PA 17601
(717) 569-0401
www.landisvalleymuseum.org
The Landis Valley Museum is a living history museum whose catalog features more than 200 heirlooms grown at the farm.

Heritage Harvest Seed
Box 2177, Carman, MB, R0G 0J0 CANADA
Tel: (204) 745-6489 / Fax: (204) 745-6489
email: heritageharvestseed@hotmail.com
Specializing in rare and endangered varieties of intriguing heirlooms.

Nichols Garden Nursery
1190 Old Salem Road NE, Albany, OR 97321-4580
(800) 422-3985 / Fax: (800) 231-5306
www.gardennursery.com/
An intriguing assortment of new and old plants.

From Joël

To Lyndsay and Patrick Mikanowski, for having convinced me to write this book with them and for their sincere friendship.

To Grant Symon, for having enabled me to rediscover vegetables through his expert eye.

To all my friends, craftspeople, and artists in the arts of the table, for the delicious creations they produced using my vegetables for the purpose of this book.

To Françoise, for her patience, her good editorial advice, her encouragement, and for all the happiness she brings me.

To Pauline and Amandine, for their participation in this adventure.

To Danièle Thiébault, my mother, for not discouraging me from taking up this fascinating career thirty-three years ago, and for having let me "cultivate my own garden."

To my whole team, who have worked with me on all my growing experiments—for many long years for some— and for their faithful and efficient support in all the routine daily tasks.

To all my friends and customers, both individuals and those in the trade, who, through the confidence they have had in me, have helped me in my quest for good flavors and good things to eat.

To all those, near and far, who helped make this book a reality.

From Lyndsay, Patrick, and Grant

To Françoise, Amandine, Pauline, and Joël Thiébault for what they have given us: sincerity, loyalty, and the joy of good food.

To Grant Symon, for his delightful, natural vision of the vegetable patch and the kitchen, of sweet and salty. To the 40 chefs and enthusiastic amateurs for their loyalty and trust.

To the Artyg design nursery and the chief nurseryman, Christophe Auger.

To all those who work with Joël in his vegetable patch and in the market throughout the year.

To Brodie for his love of JLP's bread and to Sarah for her patience and encouragement.

To Baptiste Kieken, an assistant photographer who is always faithful, sincere, and appreciative of good food.

To Delphine Roullier, the "gofer" who got our recipes from the chefs and carefully read each text.

To Catherine Minot for her hard work.

To the Saint-Aubin family for its *joie de vivre*.

To Gisou Bavoillot for her faith and enthusiasm, which have remained intact, and not forgetting Sylvie Ramaut and Aurélie Sallandrouze.

sinar

for the images in the book using their digitization process, **Sinarback eMotion22**.

Photo credits

Cover pages: Baptiste Kieken, Marguerite Mikanowski, Patrick Mikanowski, and Grant Symon; page 13: photo Yves Jannès, Ed, Monelle Hayot; page 18: Paris, musée d'Orsay © Photo RMN/© Hervé Lewandowski; page 20: Patrick Mikanowski; page 23: left, top Patrick Mikanowski. All other photos in the book: Grant Symon.

To contact Patrick or Lyndsay Mikanowski and for more information:
www.mikanowski.com

To contact Joël Thiébault:
joel-thiebault@wanadoo.fr and for more information: **joel-thiebault.fr.st**

For more about Grant Symon:
www.GrantSymon.com

Publishing Director Ghislaine Bavoillot
Art Editor Patrick Mikanowski
English translation Josephine Bacon, American Pie
Copyediting Penelope Isaac
Proofreading Helen Adedotun
Production Elzear@wanadoo.fr
Graphics & Design Artyg@wanadoo.fr
Color Separation Reproscan

Originally published in French as *Légumes de Joël*
© Éditions Flammarion, Paris, 2005

English-language edition © Éditions Flammarion, 2006

All rights reserved. No part of this publication may be reproduced in any form or by any means, electronic, photocopy information retrieval system, or otherwise, without written permission from
Éditions Flammarion, 87, quai Panhard et Levassor
75647 Paris Cedex 13

www.editions.flammarion.com

06 07 08 4 3 2 1

FC0511-06-III
ISBN-10: 2-0803-0511-5 / ISBN-13: 9782080305114
Dépôt légal: 03/2006

Printed in Italy by Errestampa